THAT'S
THE
SPIRIT!

THAT'S THE SPIRIT!

JONATHAN RAY

100 of the world's
greatest spirits,
liqueurs and digestifs
to drink with style

Cover illustration by David Doran

Hardie Grant

QUADRILLE

"HE HAD DISCOVERED THE PRIME GRAND SECRET OF ETERNAL YOUTH – TO KEEP THE DECANTER CIRCULATING AND NEVER TO GO TO BED BEFORE FOUR IN THE MORNING."

P.G. WODEHOUSE, *FULL MOON*

CONTENTS

INTRODUCTION

We spirits lovers have never had it so good. We are in the midst of an apparently unstoppable gin revolution (in case you hadn't noticed) and on the cusp of what I predict to be a similarly irresistible rum revival. Sales of fine whisky, cognac, tequila and vodka are also soaring, craft distilleries are popping up all over the place and our collective thirst for classic and quirky cocktails shows no sign at all of abating.

I've lost count of the number of spirits-related press releases I get each day alerting me to a new brand, a new bar, a new cocktail, a new mixer or a fashionable new master or mistress of mixology keen to be quoted.

And it's all so markedly different from when I embarked on my spirits journey as a teenager way back in the seventies. My parents and their friends drank bucket-loads of hard liquor for sure and certainly far more than they did wine. Indeed, dear Uncle John, for example, didn't even drink wine. Whenever I dropped by I was offered whisky and soda or gin and tonic and that was it. If I wanted wine or even beer, I had to bring my own. Well, either that or sneak a swig or so of his cooking sherry.

The trouble was that the spirits back then really weren't that interesting. The whisky would have been Bell's or Teacher's; the gin would have been Gordon's or Booth's; and the mixers would have been Schweppes or Canada Dry. There might also have been a dusty bottle of Green Chartreuse or cherry brandy at the back of the cupboard – the tops crusty with age and impossible to open – and that was pretty much it.

At school, my mates and I would smuggle in quarter bottles of Gordon's and Smirnoff and think we were frightfully cool knocking them back behind the bike sheds, trying desperately hard not to be sick. In the holidays we'd drink Tequila Sunrises and Harvey Wallbangers but only to show off to the girls and to get drunk. I don't think any of us actually enjoyed them.

It wasn't until I started work at the wine merchant Berry Bros

& Rudd after university that I really got a taste for spirits. Berrys' had an enviable range and we were encouraged to taste whatever we fancied so that we had at least some vague idea of what we were talking about to customers.

Frapin Cognac, I remember, was an early favourite as was The King's Ginger Liqueur (both are in this book). From these I graduated to kummel – the taste for which has never left me – to single malt whisky and to fine Caribbean rum. I loved how they all spoke so clearly of where they came from.

The spirits, liqueurs and digestifs you will find in these pages – my 100 absolute favourites – are the fruits of thirty years' browsing and sluicing, initially at Berrys' and subsequently as a constantly thirsty journalist. Many of the bottles, such as Bénédictine, say, Cointreau, Courvoisier and Grand Marnier, will be familiar to you; many, such as the orange-flavoured liqueur from Martinique, the summer spirit from an island off Sweden, the single malt whisky from Switzerland and the

exquisite almond-flavoured grappa ideal for augmenting your morning espresso, probably won't be.

I've not been paid, bullied or cajoled into including any of them. The selection is mine and mine alone. I've tasted them all and drink many of them rather too regularly. I hope you seek out and try as many as you can and that you come to love them as I do. That's the spirit!

Jonathan Ray
Brighton 2018

100 SPIRITS, LIQUEURS & DIGESTIFS

The bottles in the following pages have been arranged alphabetically for ease but, of course, you can sample them in any order you like (remembering that it's never wise to mix your drinks). The especially curious barflies among you might like to find out more about particular types of spirit, liqueur or digestif, in which case I suggest you turn to page 166 where you will find them all grouped into whiskies, vodkas, gins, cognacs, etc.

I have included brands that range from the outrageously good value to the outrageously decadent – because there really is a spirit for every occasion in life.

ABSOLUT ELYX SINGLE ESTATE HANDCRAFTED VODKA SWEDEN

Ten or so years ago, in an effort to understand the subject a bit better, I arranged to taste a dozen different vodkas in the company of two industry experts – Ian Wisniewski and Tom Innes. We tasted the vodkas (including Smirnoff Black, Grey Goose, Russian Standard, Wyborowa, Belvedere and so on) blind – i.e. with the bottles covered, so we had no means of identifying them – and we tasted them in four ways: neat (at room temperature); neat (from the freezer); in a Dry Martini; and mixed with tonic. We scored each sample out of ten and then added our marks together to find the winner.

You must have been able to hear the sound of jaws crashing to the ground all of 20 miles away for the vodka that came top after seven hours' hard tasting was – you won't believe it – Glen's. You know, Glen's the supermarket vodka made not from rye or wheat nor even potato or barley but from sugar beet. Yes, *that* vodka! We were astounded. It's fair to say that the category has moved on and such a result would not be possible today. In those days vodka seemed no more than an alcohol delivery system, sold on the back of crafty marketing.

Today, there are some beautifully crafted examples around and none more so than this, a single-estate vodka from Sweden, distilled using a century-old hand-operated copper column still. This is proper sipping vodka: soft, smooth, creamy and – despite its high strength – gentle too. No need to slosh it into a cocktail, although if you do it will only enhance the concoction. Absolut suggest drinking it with one large ice cube to keep it cold but without diluting it too much.

I remember Ian Wisniewski telling me at our tasting that vodka's much more than something to get you plastered. Compared to aged spirits such as cognacs or malts, the details are much smaller, but they are there to be discovered. And this is just the vodka with which to discover them.

42.3% vol; www.absolutelyx.com

AMRUT FUSION
SINGLE MALT WHISKY INDIA

My late father was very fond of his drink. That's not to say I ever saw him drunk – I didn't – but I hardly ever saw him without a drink in his hand either.

When I was in my teens we lived in what I took to be bucolic bliss in Kent until one day Pa declared he could stand the bloody country no longer and he, my mother and I promptly upped sticks to London and the set of rooms he owned in Albany, Piccadilly. The first thing my father did was to buy several fridges – for the study, the sitting room, the dining room and the bedroom – and pack them full of bottles. He couldn't bear to be more than a yard away from refreshment. He would try anything out of academic interest but had his favourite tipples, namely Guinness, pink gin (not too bothered about the brand so long as it was served in a decent measure), Bollinger and Delamain Pale & Dry Cognac.

Often friends would bring him a bottle of something quirky to try and there was nothing quirkier than the Indian whisky he kept on the sitting-room fridge for years. It purported to come from the Royal Jodhpur Distillery and the label declared that it had been 'Distilled and Bottled at Buckingham Palace under the Personal Supervision of His Majesty King George VI'. It was vile and heaven knows where it was really made.

There's no reason why fine whisky can't be made in India, of course, and if you're in any doubt I beg you to try this astonishingly fine example from Amrut Distilleries in Bangalore. Spirits distilled from peated Scottish barley and unpeated Indian barley are aged separately in American oak before being blended (hence 'Fusion') and finished together. The result is a whisky of delightful sweet and smoky complexity. It's won many serious awards including 'World Whisky of the Year' from *Malt Advocate* and 'Third Finest Whisky in the World' from Jim Murray's *Whisky Bible*. King George VI would have loved it.

50% vol; www.amrutdistilleries.com

ANGOSTURA AROMATIC BITTERS
TRINIDAD AND TOBAGO

It's said that a cocktail cabinet without Angostura Bitters is like a kitchen without salt and pepper. It's the acme of all bitters, the finest of all flavour enhancers. Just think of the cocktails in which it's a crucial ingredient: the Pink Gin, the Old Fashioned, the Manhattan, the Champagne Cocktail, the Singapore Sling, the Mai Tai, the Pisco Sour and so on. It's not to be drunk neat; it's incredibly bitter and it's also more than a little alcoholic at almost 45% vol. All you need are a few drops and your cocktails will be transformed.

It was originally conceived as an appetite inducer and cure for stomach complaints by one Dr Johann Siegert, a young army surgeon. By 1820, Dr S was in Venezuela fighting for independence under the Great Liberator, Simón Bolívar, and was soon appointed Surgeon General of the military hospital in Guayana Region. There, Siegert started work on a herbal elixir, realizing that a loss of appetite among the soldiers could be disastrous, given that an army is said to march on its stomach. In 1824, Dr Siegert's Aromatic Bitters was born, an immediate hit in his hospital and – soon – far beyond.

Sailors who visited Venezuela took it around the world and just as the concept of cocktails began to take off in the 1850s, so Siegert started to export it commercially, and it quickly became an indispensable addition to all manner of alcoholic drinks. Siegert renamed his potion Angostura Bitters after the town in which he lived (later renamed Ciudad Bolívar) and not – as is sometimes supposed – after *Angostura trifoliata*, a medicinal plant, the bark of which is used in several bitters but not that of Siegert.

Today Angostura Bitters is produced by Siegert's descendents in Port of Spain, Trinidad, still to the original recipe. It's recognizable by its yellow cap and outsized label. If you don't have any at home, go out and buy some this very minute.

44.7% vol; www.angosturabitters.com

ANTICA FORMULA RED VERMOUTH ITALY

You like a fine Negroni, right? Oh come on! Everyone likes a fine Negroni. Even a bad Negroni is a fine Negroni. It's one of those rare cocktails that is almost impossible to screw up and is also unusual in that it can be consumed before, during or after a meal with equal pleasure.

As you know, all you need is one third each of Campari, gin and sweet red vermouth. Lob in some ice and the zest or a slice of orange and – bingo! – there you are in clover. Crikey, you can even attempt my signature pudding and make a Negroni jelly.

A friend of mine calls it the 'Airport Cocktail', since even the humblest hostelry encountered on one's travels – such as grotty pub, airport lounge or bar – will have the nuts and bolts required to create something palatable. The worst that can happen is that the vermouth might be a touch oxidized.

But if even a bad Negroni can be a fine Negroni, the perfect Negroni should be spectacular. You can't muck about with the Campari, of course, but you can ensure you have a tip-top gin and the best red vermouth available. As for the latter, I humbly suggest that you look no further than this.

Made in small batches in Milan by Fratelli Branca to Antonio Benedetto Carpano's original 250-year-old recipe of Italian white wines, top-quality vanilla beans and a mix of aromatic herbs and plants, it's wonderfully bitter/sweet, citrusy, raisiny, clove-rich and complex. The replica bottle (each one of which is numbered) and antique label look wonderful and every home should have one.

Beyond the Negroni, it's an essential ingredient in such classic cocktails as the Americano, Manhattan, Sbagliato and Hanky Panky and is pretty damn fine served on its own over ice with a slice of orange.

16.5% vol; www.carpano.com

APPENZELLER SINGLE MALT SÄNTIS SWISS ALPINE WHISKY EDITION HIMMELBERG SWITZERLAND

So there I was in Appenzell in northeast Switzerland. I had just arrived and was sitting quietly in the sunshine enjoying some excellent local beer from the Locher Brauerei. And then I saw it. I thought I'd had too much to drink and was imagining it. But I hadn't and I wasn't.

The chocolate-box-pretty buildings around me were bedecked with flags. There was the familiar Swiss flag and the unfamiliar (to me) Appenzell flag, which I could now see displayed the canton's coat of arms, that of a large black bear on its hind legs with red claws and – I don't know how else to put this – a monstrous red erection. It was impossible to miss.

Appenzell is the smallest, most traditional and most old-fashioned of all the Swiss cantons, with elections and matters of import still decided by a show of hands in the town square. Hitherto, it's been best known for the Appenzeller mountain dog, the tangy Appenzeller cheese and for the fact that women only won the right to vote here as recently as 1991. To this list I would like to add the proudly priapic bear (do Google it if you don't believe me), the extremely toothsome Appenzeller beer and the very fine Appenzeller Single Malt, both made by the Locher family.

I had come across the beer before. The Hanfblüte (hemp) beer is particularly fine in a heady, cannabis sort of way, as is the Vollmond beer, brewed only during a full moon. The whisky, though, was new to me (it only launched in 2002) and I was instantly smitten.

There's the smoky, earthy, spicy Edition Dreifaltigkeit; the vanilla-laden Edition Sigel, aged in small beer casks; and a wonderful apricot malt liqueur. My favourite though, is this, the Edition Himmelberg, aged in a mix of beer and wine casks. It's soft and smooth with an elegant and seductive fruitiness to it and it was a worthy winner of a silver medal at the 2016 International Wine & Spirit Competition.

The label even has a picture of the aforementioned bear, although this time he's coyly hiding his, erm, excitement behind a well-placed heraldic shield.

43% vol; www.saentismalt.com

"WHISKY IS LIQUID SUNSHINE."

GEORGE BERNARD SHAW

APPLETON ESTATE 21 YEAR OLD RUM
JAMAICA

It was a while back, in Pollen Street Social in London's West End, that I first had a rum Negroni. I couldn't think what to have and the bartender suggested it. I'd never had one before – it had never occurred to me that such a thing existed – and I was immediately, wantonly seduced. Instead of the usual gin, the bartender had used Appleton Estate Signature Blend Rum and, oh my goodness, it was delicious.

The elusive notes of toffee, vanilla and dark brown sugar the rum offered were cleverly held in check by the bitter Seville orange tang of the Campari, which somehow, at the same time, echoed the rum's caramelized, candied orange notes. The tangy sweet red vermouth then brought it all together. It was a merry, tongue-tingling dance that was played out in my mouth.

Keen to learn more about this wonderful, drink-changing rum, I decided to trade up and had a glass neat of this, Appleton Estate's 21 Year Old. Well, that's me ruined forever. It's stunningly fine. I just wish it wasn't so damn expensive.

They've been making hand-crafted rums at Appleton Estate in the Nassau Valley in the heart of Jamaica since 1749 (and quite possibly since 1655) and this is the perfect example of top-quality sipping rum. Made from molasses under the guidance of Joy Spence, the first female Master Blender in the world, it's aged in American oak barrels for a minimum 21 years, is sold in individually numbered, limited edition bottles and is utterly exquisite.

I adore its mellow softness and its deep, toffee-rich, nutty, orangey and even slightly peppery flavours, and its long, dry finish. If ever you're looking for a post-prandial alternative to a fine single malt, cognac or armagnac, then – so long as you've got the dough – there's no need to look any further.

43% vol; www.appletonestate.com

ARDBEG 10 YEAR OLD SINGLE MALT SCOTCH WHISKY SCOTLAND

There's a definite salty tang to the whiskies of Ardbeg. Hardly surprising, given the distillery's proximity to the sea. Dammit, sometimes when the weather is really wild on the craggy southern shores of the Isle of Islay, Ardbeg is almost in the sea, so close is it. But it's not so much the saltiness as the peatiness of Ardbeg that grabs you.

I remember when I first visited the glory that is Ardbeg I asked distillery manager Mickey Heads some rambling and ill-informed question about the importance of peat and what it gave to his whisky. He wordlessly led me straight into a brightly whitewashed former malt bin and told me to breathe in. I almost choked. The place reeked of the stuff which, given that it hadn't been used as a malt bin for over 30 years, gave me some idea of the influence that peat can have.

The peat here is grassy and mossy, mixed with heather, wood, sand and even seaweed. In its raw state it doesn't smell at all but, once lit, it releases a wonderfully rich, earthy aroma that is replicated in the whisky itself. And as for that iodine and salt I also detected, Heads simply waved his hand towards the aforementioned briny breaking on the cobbles of the old jetty, yards from where we stood. I was beginning to grasp that Heads was a man of few words when a gesture will do.

Ardbeg 10 Year Old (non-chill filtered with a strength of 46% vol for maximum flavour) is a wonder and about as peaty, as smoky and as complex as you can get. But it's supremely balanced too, with a beguiling sweetness to it, and if you're a peat-head you will simply lap it up. If you're not, well, maybe it ain't for you. But don't feel too bad because there are folk out there who would bite your hand off for a bottle. So much so, in fact, that Ardbeg (owned by Glenmorangie, by the way, and thus by extension, LVMH) recently announced plans to double its production capacity in order to cope with demand.

46% vol; www.ardbeg.com

BAILEYS IRISH CREAM LIQUEUR IRELAND

Love it or loathe it (and many – my wife included – love it whilst professing to loathe it), Baileys Irish Cream is the best-selling liqueur in the world. It's a phenomenal success. Indeed, a rough estimate suggests that some 12 billion glasses of it have been poured since its creation in 1973 by David Dand, of Gilbey's of Ireland, and advertising executives, Hugh Reade Seymour-Davies and David Gluckman. These last two were tasked by International Distillers & Vintners to come up with a new drink for Gilbey's to export and were paid £3,000 for their trouble.

The bottle might say that it's produced by R&A Bailey & Co, but that's a complete fiction, being an amalgam of Baileys Bistro in Greek Street, Soho, near where Seymour-Davies and Gluckman worked, and the Royal & Ancient Golf Club (the R & A) about which Gluckman was reading when he had a eureka moment. In truth, Baileys is made and owned by multi-national drinks company Diageo.

Fresh cream (collected every day from 1,500 Irish farms and 40,000 cows known as the Baileys Ladies), triple pot-still distilled Irish whiskey, neutral white spirit, vanilla, chocolate and sugar are the liqueur's only ingredients, the concept being based on the Brandy Alexander. The initial target was to sell 150,000 cases, but by year two they were selling 300,000 and it's fair to say they've never looked back, with current annual sales of around seven million cases.

Cream makes up half of every bottle and by using a patented process based on ice cream technology, protein is first taken out of the cream before being replaced somehow (don't ask me, I've no idea). This gives the cream a positive charge and when negatively charged alcohol is introduced to the mix, it envelops the cream, acting as a preservative. So it is that Baileys, unlike any other cream liqueur, needs no other preservative and boasts a shelf-life of two years once opened. Funnily enough, though, despite my wife's protestations, the shelf life in our house is a bare two hours.

17% vol; www.baileys.com

BALCONES BRIMSTONE TEXAS SCRUB OAK SMOKED CORN WHISKY USA

When I worked at Berry Bros & Rudd in St. James's Street, London, all those years ago, scores of tourists would visit us. They loved the fact the company had been founded in 1698 and was still family-owned, and that the wood-panelled shop (which had no bottles on display even though it was, erm, a wine shop) had barely changed over the centuries. They would stare at us as we sat in our pin-stripes at vast desks writing orders out in long-hand. No, we didn't have quills, but might just as well have. If they were lucky, they might catch us playing cricket on the shop's famously sloping floor or find us engaging in our favourite pastime: ignore-the-customer-by-pretending-to-be-on-the-phone-and-see-who-cracks-first.

Americans loved it, of course, Texans more than anyone because – as a plaque on the wall outside recorded – the first floor of the building had been home to the Texas Legation from 1842–45. I remember once being bearded by a vast Stetson-sporting Texan who wanted his photo taken next to the plaque. He explained that they didn't make wine back where he was from but if they ever got round to it, it would undoubtedly be the best in the world. I didn't really feel I could argue with that.

I believe they do make wine in Texas these days although I've not tried any. What they do make is whisky – really, really good whisky. None make it better than Balcones in Waco, founded in 2008 by craft distilling genius Chip Tate. Sadly Chip had a spat with his investors and has since left the company. His legacy remains though and the whiskies are exceptional. They're not bourbons, but proudly Texan whiskies. This big, brash, beast of a whisky is the quirkiest in an already quirky range. Made from roasted blue corn, the whisky itself is then smoked (I know, nor me) and tastes like no other spirit I've ever had. If whisky – or just Texas – is your thing, you have to try it.

53% vol; www.balconesdistilling.com

21

BEEFEATER 24 GIN ENGLAND

The first gin I ever drank was Gordon's. The first gin I ever enjoyed was Beefeater. In the summer of 1976 I was 16 and, having failed most of my O Levels, I spent my time getting into mischief at the Marquee Club in Wardour Street. It was, after all, a memorable year for music lovers.

Cracky, a sometime roadie with Led Zep, Van der Graaf Generator and the like, was the Marquee's greeter and would let me and my schoolmates in for free and would ply us with endless large glasses of Gordon's Gin and Rose's Lime. Cracky was unabashedly gay and would lurk close by, waiting for the gin to take effect. He would then amble off in half-hearted pursuit, particularly of Kim but once of Johnny – a future peer of the realm – who, on one memorable evening (9 July 1976; I still have the live EP), having courteously batted away Cracky's not-very-serious attentions, mistook the door to the stage as being that to the exit and suddenly found himself tumbling over Eddie and the Hot Rods, mid-song, much to his and the band's bewilderment and the cacophonous delight of the audience.

My dear Uncle John later weaned me off Gordon's 'n' Rose's ('a pimp's drink') onto Beefeater and tonic ('a drinker's drink') and I grew to love it.

Beefeater manages to be both traditional and innovative thanks to the much-loved veteran head distiller Desmond Payne who was recently awarded an MBE for his gin mastery. (Note to whoever decides such things: what took you so long and why wasn't it a CBE at least?)

Beefeater 24 is a marvellous gin made from 12 botanicals including grapefruit peel, lemon peel, coriander, almond, Japanese Sencha tea and Chinese green tea infused in spirit for 24 hours. It's remarkably smooth and citrusy and full of character. It's great with a fine tonic, of course, and brilliant in cocktails too. I'd skip the Rose's Lime though.

45% vol; www.beefeatergin.com

BELSAZAR WHITE VERMOUTH GERMANY

When I worked at Oddbins as a gap year student some – oh good grief – 40 years ago, we stocked just two brands of vermouth: Cinzano and Martini. And, incidentally, we stocked just four gins: Gordon's, White Satin (what became of that?), Booth's (it went kaput last year) and Beefeater. Who would have thought, back then, that we would now have scores of different vermouths to choose from and hundreds of gins? And what about mixers? Back in the late seventies there were just Schweppes, Rawlings and Canada Dry. The alcoholic landscape is changing so fast and we have undergone what I can only term a Glorious Revolution. We drinkers have never had it so good.

Belsazar – launched by entrepreneurs Maximillian Wagner and Sebastian Brack in 2013 and quickly snapped up by Diageo – is one of the hippest of new vermouths on the market and has already seduced a thirsty public with its four core expressions – red, rosé, dry and white – and its limited editions such as Riesling and Vintage Rosé.

I love the whole range but if I had to choose one, it would be this, the Belsazar White Vermouth. Produced in Germany's Black Forest at the family-owned Alfred Schladerer Distillery, it has as its base some fine German Gewurztraminer wine from the vineyards Kaiserstuhl and Markgräflerland. This is sweetened with grape juice and flavoured with a couple of dozen botanicals steeped in neutral spirit. Then – and this is the key to Belsazar's unique profile – some of Alfred Schladerer's fabled fruit brandies are added before the vermouth is blended, rested in stone jars, filtered and bottled.

It makes for an astoundingly fine drink, full of fresh peaches, pears, herbs and vanilla. I like to drink it with some basil leaves and fresh lime, muddled in a glass and served over crushed ice (a sort of faux Caipirinha) or topped up with tonic, ice and a slice of orange. It's simple and absurdly fine.

18% vol; www.belsazar.com

BELVEDERE SINGLE ESTATE RYE VODKA
POLAND

You probably think we drinks writers have it cushy. Nothing could be further from the truth. I mean, there are only so many bottling lines you can visit; only so many gins or newly fermented Pinot Noirs you can taste at 8.30A.M. with a hangover; only so many liver function tests you can have. It requires resolve and fortitude, I can tell you.

Occasionally, though, a pale shaft of sunlight pierces through the gloom and makes our struggles worthwhile. I refer in this instance to being invited to sample the late, lamented Belvedere Private Room. This was a wheeze dreamt up by Belvedere Vodka whereby customers could book an evening's entertainment in their own home for up to a dozen guests. Staying in was the new going out. The Belvedere team came and set up a bar in our garden where two barmen proceeded to mix an endless number of martinis. There was a manicurist and a make-up artist in our living room; a masseuse in our playroom; and a poker dealer, complete with green baize table, in our dining room. We had a veritable hoot.

I'll never forget passing my chum Mark in the hall. Having just won a couple of hands of cards and downed a trio of martinis, he was off for a massage. 'Oh my God,' he sighed. 'This is the best night of my life. I don't think I've ever been so happy.' I've had a distinct fondness for Belvedere ever since.

Although the Belvedere Private Room is no more, their vodkas continue to impress. In autumn 2017 they launched their Single Estate Rye Series with two vodkas made using rare Diamond Dankowskie Rye but with very different terroirs: Smogóry Forest in the west of Poland and Lake Bartezek in the northeast. The one is full-flavoured, creamy and slightly salty; the other is light, delicate and floral. Both are absolutely first rate and deserve to be sipped slowly, neat and ice cold, rather than sloshed into cocktails. The masseuse can wait.

40% vol; www.belvederevodka.com

BÉNÉDICTINE FRANCE

Ok, fingers on buzzers. Who or what is the biggest single consumer of Bénédictine, the celebrated French liqueur? No, no, don't Google it, you'll spoil the fun.

The French Parliament? No. The French Foreign Legion? No. The Court of Henri, Grand Duke of Luxembourg? Nope. Gosh, I dunno, let me take a wild guess, erm, how about Burnley Miners' Social Club in Lancashire, UK? Yes, well done! I knew you'd get it.

Bénédictine, now part of the giant Bacardi portfolio, has been made at Fécamp, on the Normandy coast of France since 1863. Wine merchant Alexandre Le Grand is said to have stumbled upon a medieval recipe for the herbal liqueur dating from 1510 in the library of Fécamp's Benedictine Abbey. He set about recreating it with the help of a local pharmacist, using several distillations of 27 herbs and spices including arnica, cinnamon, coriander, juniper, lemon balm, myrrh, nutmeg and saffron. It's sweetened, not with sugar, but with honey, and the exact recipe is a closely guarded secret.

Some folk reckon that Le Grand made up the guff about discovering the recipe and simply traded on the mythology of the monks at the local abbey and came up with the formula himself. Either way, Le Grand built the Palais Bénédictine for the liqueur's manufacture – where it's still made today – and was knighted by the Pope for his trouble.

But back to Burnley where the Miners' Club gets through a reported 1,000 bottles a year and Burnley Football club around 30 bottles per home match. It all started in World War One when the East Lancashire Regiment was stationed near Fécamp. The troops got a taste for the local liqueur and would regularly drink it diluted with hot water to keep them warm and a little bit squiffy. Known as a Bene'n'hot, it's still drunk this way in Burnley today, although younger folk are said to favour it mixed with Red Bull as a Bene Bomb, the local alternative to the ghastly Jäger Bomb.

40% vol; www.benedictinedom.com

BENROMACH 15 YEAR OLD SPEYSIDE SINGLE MALT SCOTCH WHISKY SCOTLAND

Benromach, in Forres, Morayshire, is the first distillery you come to on Scotland's so-called Malt Whisky Trail and it's a sweet spot and no mistake. But blink and you'll miss it, for it's the smallest working distillery in all Speyside. It takes just three men to operate (two distillers and a general manager) and produces barely 1,000 casks a year, but what casks they are!

The distillery was established in 1898 but fell into disuse and was closed many times before being resurrected in 1998 by the family-owned malt whisky specialists, Gordon & MacPhail. Since then it's gone from strength to strength.

So small is Benromach, though, that a wander around the distillery – taking in the barley grinder, the mash tuns, the wooden washbacks, the two copper stills, the spirit safe, the filling room and the slumbering casks of spirit in the bonded warehouse – takes mere moments. All of which suits me fine because it means there's more time for a few drams.

I've always enjoyed the spicy, rich fruit character of Benromach and its trademark touch of delicate smoke, which is so unusual for a modern Speyside single malt but which harks back to a style of yesteryear. There are no computers, not even pressure gauges, and the team boast proudly that everything is 'hand-controlled by touch, feel, smell and experience'.

They use pure spring water; medium peated malted barley (for that elegant smoky character); and distiller's and brewer's yeast (for a rich, full fermentation). And they're big on their wood finishes; the current range including a Château Cissac finish, a Hermitage finish and a Sassicaia finish. I wish they still made the deliciously rich and creamy Tokaji finish. That was a real peach.

The current expression that most hits the spot for me, though, is this, the 15 Year Old. Matured in a mix of bourbon and sherry casks, it has a remarkable array of aromas and flavours including honey, smoke, chocolate, spice, citrus and goodness knows what else. It shows off different facets every time I return to it and it's an absolute joy.

43% vol; www.benromach.com

"I ALWAYS TAKE SCOTCH WHISKY AT NIGHT AS A PREVENTIVE OF TOOTHACHE. I HAVE NEVER HAD THE TOOTHACHE; AND WHAT IS MORE, I NEVER INTEND TO HAVE IT."

MARK TWAIN

BEPI TOSOLINI SALIZÁ AMARETTO VENEZIANO LIQUEUR ITALY

Having drunk long and having drunk deep, we all got a bit toxyboo last Christmas. No surprise there, you might say. Oi, cheeky! Anyway, having exhausted the crackers and their appalling riddles, we turned inevitably to the traditional (in our house anyway) liqueur chocolates and Lazzaroni Amaretti biscuits.

It was only a matter of time, of course, before Mrs Ray fell back on that hallowed, pissed-person-in-an-Italian-restaurant tradition of lighting the biscuits' wafer-thin wrappers and watching them burn and soar to the ceiling. The kids loved it, betting on whose would fly highest. The kids loved the biscuits too, while the grown-ups loved this sublime amaretto brought by a kind cousin.

I always thought that both amaretti and amaretto were made from almonds, like the marzipan they both taste similar to. It turns out that amaretti, which come from Saronno in Lombardy, are made from ground apricot kernels (which I always thought were poisonous but aren't, apparently, when cooked) along with sugar and egg white. Which is all very odd because this amaretto from the family-owned distillery of Bepi Tosolini (currently celebrating its 75th anniversary) tastes just like them and is made from almonds. Sorry, splitting hairs, I know – I was just curious.

Anyway, there are certainly better-known amaretto liqueurs than this but there are definitely none better. Where other examples can be unbalanced – too sweet or too bitter and too likely to have been made using concentrates or extracts –

28

this is perfectly judged and produced in a truly artisanal and traditional way.

They start by macerating almonds in alcohol for a week or so. The result is distilled in an alembic still and then blended with a touch of sugar, caramel (to ensure consistency of colour) and a few hearty splashes of fine aged brandy just to add a bit more get up and go. Nothing bogus or artificial is added and it's as natural and genuine a process as possible.

If amaretto is your thing (and it's mine) you simply won't find a better one. It knocks its rivals right out of the park and I now won't drink any other.

28% vol; www.bepitosolini.it

"DRINK BECAUSE YOU ARE HAPPY, BUT NEVER BECAUSE YOU ARE MISERABLE."

G.K. CHESTERTON, *HERETICS*

BERRYS' NO. 3 GIN HOLLAND

I don't know if you know Dukes in London's West End? It's a small, desperately discreet hotel tucked away in a miniscule cul-de-sac off St. James's Street. I used to spend far more time there than was good for me. Well, when I say 'there' I really mean the fabled Dukes Bar. I don't think I've ever so much as poked my nose round any other door in the hotel. The only part I (and many others) have eyes for, is said bar.

These days, this elegantly hushed retreat – the antithesis of the brash, noisy, modern cocktail bar – is presided over by Alessandro Palazzi, a veritable maestro of mixology. He knows the history and the background of every classic cocktail you can think of, and most of those that you can't, and he wields a mean Boston shaker.

The signature cocktail is the Dry Martini and although Palazzi might have relaxed the Dukes Bar dress code a bit, the two-Martinis-only rule still applies. It's just so damn potent and too many guests were knocking them back with abandon, standing up too quickly and finding that the walls had rather fine hand-woven carpets attached to them.

I love these Martinis and although I might once have managed two I find now that one is plenty. The key to their success is the gin Palazzi uses: Berrys' No. 3 Gin. This exceptional, whistle-clean spirit is made with just six botanicals: juniper, orange peel, grapefruit peel, angelica, coriander and cardamom. Berry Bros & Rudd (whose shop at No. 3 St. James's Street gives the gin its name and is just yards away from Dukes) devised the gin's recipe and it's made for them by De Kuyper Royal Distillers in Holland.

Palazzi pours one teaspoon of Italian vermouth into a frozen glass and coats it in a circular motion. He adds 85ml (2¾fl oz) of ice-cold Berrys' No. 3 Gin and the zest of an Amalfi lemon.

Sip slowly and enjoy. Oh, and don't stand up in a rush.

46% vol; www.no3gin.com

COCKTAILS THROUGH THE AGES

One of the highlights of my cocktail-drinking career was being served the driest of Dry Martinis by the legendary barman Hoy Wong (known as Mr Hoy) at the Algonquin Hotel in New York. He's over 101 years old as I write and had just passed 90 when he served me.

Mr Hoy and the Algonquin were my links to a glittering cocktail-drenched past. As you know, the hotel was famous as the 1920s home of the 'Vicious Circle', whose members included such barbed wits and doughty drinkers as Dorothy Parker, Robert Benchley, Harpo Marx and George S. Kaufman. The fabled Round Table at which they sat is still in use and may have been the table Miss Parker was referring to when she quipped: 'I like to have a martini, two at the very most. After three I'm under the table, after four I'm under my host.'

I got quite a frisson as Mr Hoy, who had made martinis for the likes of Julie London, Marilyn Monroe, Bob Hope, Judy Garland, Frank Sinatra, Danny Kaye et al made one for me, using plenty of Tanqueray Gin and not much Noilly Prat. It was perfect.

I was in New York on the orders of my editor at the *Daily Telegraph* – where I was then drinks editor – to come up with some guff concerning the 200th anniversary of the first definitive example of the word 'cocktail' being used to mean an alcoholic drink. Yet another punishing assignment…

In May 1806, Harry Crosswell, editor of *The Balance and Columbian Repository* responded to the question 'What is a cocktail?' by explaining that it was '… a stimulating liquor, composed of spirits of any kind, sugar, water and bitters… it renders the heart stout and bold, at the same time that it fuddles the head.'

I attempted to experience as many such concoctions as I could, chronologically. I started with the Old Fashioned from the 1880s and then moved to the Widow's Kiss, an all but forgotten cocktail from the 1890s comprised of calvados, Bénédictine, Green Chartreuse and a dash or so of Angostura Bitters.

This was followed by the Bronx cocktail (gin, sweet red vermouth, dry white vermouth, fresh orange juice) from the 1900s, notorious as the drink that supposedly sent Bill W(ilson) so far over the edge that he co-founded Alcoholics Anonymous.

From the 1910s, it was a French 75 (gin, fresh lemon juice and champagne), created in 1915 and so-named because it was said to have the kick of a French 75mm field gun. Mr Hoy's sublime Martini represented the 1920s, thanks to which I only made it as far as the 1930s with a Margarita at the Pegu Club.

Once my head is a touch less fuddled, I will return and pick up where I left off.

BOBBY'S SCHIEDAM JENEVER HOLLAND

When in Amsterdam, there are few greater pleasures than sitting in one of the old taverns on one of the great canals and toying with a fine beer and a plate of *ossenworst*, that delectable raw beef sausage the locals so love, and simply watching the world go by.

If you feel brave enough you can up the ante a bit and treat yourself to a *kopstoot* (literal translation: headbutt), an ancient Dutch tradition whereby you knock back in one a tulip-shaped glass of jenever and extinguish the fire, so to speak, with a large glass of ice-cold beer. If you're feeling a tad more decorous, sip at the glasses alternately, savouring the contrasting alcoholic and flavour sensations and, after a brace more, the increased lack of feeling in your legs.

Jenever – first created in Holland in the sixteenth century – is the precursor to English gin. Having nicked the recipe for so-called 'Dutch Courage' off them, we tweaked it a bit. Both spirits are flavoured with juniper but they remain very different, with jenever more like a juniper-flavoured whisky and English gin more like juniper-flavoured vodka.

In Holland they triple distil (in a pot still) a mix of cereals to get what they call malt wine. This is then blended with grain or sugar beet vodka (re-distilled with juniper and various other botanicals) to create jenever.

The House of Herman Jansen, a family-owned distillery in Schiedam, has been producing fine spirits since 1777 and it's here that they make Bobby's Schiedam Jenever, launched in 2016. In a case of East meets West, it's a blend of traditional Dutch malt wine and Indonesian botanicals such as juniper (of course), cubeb pepper, cardamom, lemongrass and ginger, all of them organic. They recommend drinking it neat from that tulip glass and so tasty is it there's no need for a subsequent large glass of beer. If you have to mix it at all, I suggest serving it over ice with some fine ginger ale and a sprig of mint. A side plate of *ossenworst* is optional.

38% vol; www.bobbysdrygin.com

DOMAINE BOINGNÈRES BAS ARMAGNAC CÉPAGES NOBLES FRANCE

The last time I drank this was in the company of some very dashing musketeers. Much to my astonishment and delight, I had been invited by the Compagnie des Mousquetaires d'Armagnac – the very jolly fraternity that promotes the delights of armagnac – to join their merry band at a great knees-up in the medieval cloisters of Condom.

We drained glass upon glass of Pousse Rapière (a fabulous cocktail of armagnac, sparkling wine and orange zest) before we inductees were introduced to the body of the hall with flaming torches and a brief biography. A sash of royal blue, complete with enamel cross, was placed around my shoulders; I signed a leather-bound register and received a parchment and a spirity kiss on both cheeks in return. The capitaine d'honneur spoke so fast that I could barely catch a word he was saying but it seemed to be along the lines that I was a good egg, that I could drink as much free armagnac as I wanted for life and that whenever I was passing through I could have my wicked way with as many of their wives and daughters as I could manage. Or something like that.

Everyone slapped me on the back and, amid loud cheers and much raising of glasses, I was led back to my chair where a bottle of this wonderful stuff was thrust into my hand: it was mine for the evening and I wasn't to leave until it was empty.

Domaine Boingnères was founded in 1807 and is one of the region's great names, run by Martine Lafitte, the sixth generation of her family to have the role. The estate concentrates on using the Folle Blanche grape variety grown in vineyards in Bas Armagnac only. The armagnacs are aged in a mix of charred new oak and old oak barrels and they come out big and powerful. At 48% vol, this example is a much higher strength than is usual for the region, which might explain my sorry disarray when I last drank it.

48% vol; sadly no website

33

BOTTEGA RISERVA PRIVATA BARRICATA GRAPPA ITALY

Family-owned Italian winemaker and distiller Bottega (not to be confused with luxury goods company Bottega Veneta) makes one heck of a lot of booze. I first got to know Bottega through their excellent Proseccos, of which they make 18 different examples and which, despite their bling packaging, are beacons of quality in an increasingly dreary category. And they're hugely popular too, sold all over the world.

I then discovered Bottega's vast range of spirits and liqueurs. There's gin, there's vermouth, there's bitters and there's all manner of sweet, cream- and grappa-based liqueurs such as Crema di Pistacchi di Sicilia (looks a bit like shampoo); Latte Machiatto Crema di Caffè e Grappa (conditioner) and Fior di Latte Cioccolato Bianco e Grappa (face mask). These are not really my thing but whenever I offer them to guests, they're gone in a trice. As for the non-cream-based liqueurs, the Bottega Pera & Grappa, made from pear juice, grappa and sugar, is utterly delicious, as is the blueberry Mirtillo.

It's Bottega's straight grappas, though, that really appeal. There are a dozen in the company's Alexander range alone, including those made from the pomace (the gunk left after winemaking) of Merlot, Chardonnay and Moscato. And they even produce a scent bottle atomizer filled with grappa, the better to spray on your oysters, say; your coffee; your cigar or, if desperate, yourself.

The Bottega Riserva Privata Barricata Grappa is easily my favourite. Produced from the pomace of the partially sun-dried Rondinella and Corvina grapes that make Amarone della Valpolicella – that wonderful, famously alcoholic red wine of the Veneto – it's aged for ten years in small oak barrels. The result is a darkly hued, richly flavoured grappa of real character. Enjoy it as you would a fine cognac or single malt. Spray it upon yourself only if you must.

43% vol; www.bottegaspa.com

BRIGHTON GIN ENGLAND

Ok, I must declare an interest here straight away, being one of the co-founders of Brighton Gin. I hope you will forgive me; it is, after all, one of my favourite spirits.

The bunch of us who launched Brighton Gin in late 2014 did so because we love Brighton and, well, we love gin. Our MD, the broadcaster and leading Pink and Rainbow Lister, Kathy Caton, had a eureka moment during an early morning run along the sea front. She realized that, despite having spent most of the previous night drowning in gin and not having gone to bed until 3A.M., she felt remarkably unscathed. Gin was clearly a very forgiving spirit and what Brighton – a hard partying town – needed, she reasoned, was such a spirit of its own. She promptly registered the name. Dotted around town, the rest of us were having similar thoughts. Somehow we all found each other and joined forces. I borrowed a vacuum still from a moonshine-making chum and we started trialling recipes on ourselves and our friends.

We now have a proper still and make our gin in small batches of 354 bottles a time, using botanicals such as fresh orange and lime peel, locally grown coriander and milk thistle (well known for its friendly attitude to one's liver). Everything is done by hand, from hand-peeling fruit for the distillation to bottling; from waxing to labelling the bottles (step forward, please, Kathy's mum, Jude), using the exact same colour as Brighton's sea-front railings.

Blowsy, buxom Brighton is a wonderful place. Somehow the sea, the Downs, the jaunty architecture, the dirty weekend-ness and the Graham Greene-ness of the place combine to create a town of relaxed tolerance where having fun is serious business. A town seemingly full of gin drinkers whom, I'm delighted to say, need frequent topping up. Our fellow Brightonians have been nothing if not supportive of our – their – gin. But as we state on the label: it's made for free thinkers and good time girls and boys *everywhere*.

40% vol; www.brightongin.com

BRUICHLADDICH, THE CLASSIC LADDIE ISLAY SINGLE MALT SCOTCH WHISKY
SCOTLAND

So, the single malt whiskies of Islay are all about peat, right? Erm, well, no actually, they're not. At least The Classic Laddie from Bruichladdich (brew-clad-y) ain't.

I love this whisky for many reasons, not least because it's not what one expects. Where the other mighty malts of Islay – Ardbeg, Bowmore, Caol Ila, Lagavulin, Laphroaig and so on – reek of peat, this stops one in one's tracks for not having one whiff or whisper of the stuff. It seems to fly in the face of everything one knows about Islay. Even the striking opaque sea green/Cambridge blue bottle is pointedly different.

Bruichladdich was founded in 1881 by brothers William, John and Robert Harvey but was mothballed many times over the following decades before being rescued from oblivion by wine merchant Mark Reynier and a group of investors in 2000. Crucially, they managed to entice the genius that is master distiller Jim McEwan (since retired) from neighbouring Bowmore to join them. Bruichladdich has subsequently become part of the Rémy Cointreau group and is where the excellent Botanist Gin is made.

It's all delightfully homespun. When I last visited, the boiler had just broken, the yeast fridge had packed up and they had just run out of water. But they managed, because it's all very hands-on. Caol Ila down the road is fully automated and it takes just six people to produce some 6.5 million bottles a year. Here, it's fully analogue and it takes 60 people to make 1.5 million bottles per annum on the original Victorian equipment.

Oh, and I should point out that they do make heavily peated whiskies here, too (the Port Charlotte range), and super heavily peated ones as well (the Octomore range), but as far as I'm concerned, this – the distillery's signature bottling – is far and away the best of its output.

Produced from 100 per cent Scottish barley (much of it grown on Islay), it's trickle distilled with minimal intervention and aged on the island in American and French oak casks. It's floral, elegantly fruity, creamy, nutty and slightly saline and, as they themselves say, as smooth as pebbles in a pool.

50% vol; www.bruichladdich.com

"FIRST YOU TAKE A DRINK, THEN THE DRINK TAKES A DRINK, THEN THE DRINK TAKES YOU."

F. SCOTT FITZGERALD

"MY OWN EXPERIENCE HAS BEEN THAT THE TOOLS I NEED FOR MY TRADE ARE PAPER, TOBACCO, FOOD, AND A LITTLE WHISKEY."

WILLIAM FAULKNER

BUSHMILLS BLACK BUSH IRISH WHISKEY NORTHERN IRELAND

I love Northern Ireland. I love the scenery (the Antrim coast is as striking and as wild a place as you will see); I love the people; I love the craic and I love the whiskey, the blended Bushmills Black Bush best of all.

I first got a taste for it whilst visiting family in County Down. It was my cousin's 40th and nobody drew a sober breath for days. We drank ridiculous amounts of Guinness chased down with doubles of Black Bush and I couldn't get enough of it. The wheels finally came off, though, in the Dufferin Arms in Killyleagh. Some rascal encouraged me to move from Black Bush onto his homemade *poitín* and that, dear reader, was that. Next thing, I was waking up three days later, stark naked on the floor of the honeymoon suite of a rather plush hotel in Dublin. I was alone and nobody has ever come forward with compromising photos so I can only assume I kept my dignity intact. How I got there remains a mystery best left unexplored.

I should have stuck to Black Bush, which, despite said misadventure, I still adore. They had been making whiskey in the village of Bushmills, County Antrim, for many years before King James I granted the Old Bushmills Whiskey Distillery its licence to distil in 1608. It is now acknowledged to be the oldest licensed whiskey distillery in the world. But as Colum Egan, Bushmills' Master Distiller, once told me, 'We're not good because we're old; we're old because we're good.'

At the heart of Black Bush are triple-distilled malt whiskeys aged in bourbon and oloroso casks to give Black Bush its signature fruity notes and intense character. The triple distillation gives lightness whilst seasoned oak adds colour and elicits hints of nuts, spice, almonds and vanilla. Egan calls it his 'loveable rogue'. It's bigger and bolder than the Bushmills Original but it's delicate too and, as Egan says, it seems to float on your tongue without touching it.

40% vol; www.bushmills.com

CAMPARI ITALY

It might have its imitators but there's nothing quite like Campari, the exquisite Milanese bitters whose blend of aromatic herbs, plants and fruit in alcohol and water hasn't changed since it was created by Gaspare Campari in 1860. These days only three people know the secret recipe with its 60 natural ingredients, and so secret is it that nobody knows who those three people are. Talk about cloak and dagger.

Gaspare Campari (1828–82) was the tenth child of a simple farmer. At 14 he started work as a waiter and became obsessed by people's drinking habits. Before long he had opened his own bar. So successful was this, he opened another in the heart of Milan, making his own cordials, cream liqueurs and bitters in the basement. His choice of location in the shadow of the Duomo was serendipitous, coinciding as it did with the opening of the Galleria Vittorio Emanuele. His bar was soon the most fashionable in town, favoured by the Milanese intelligentsia, and his bitters – then called 'Bitter all'Uso d'Holanda' – the most sought-after of drinks.

Today Gruppo Campari is a massive concern, which owns such major brands as Glen Grant, Cinzano, Wild Turkey, Appleton Estate and Grand Marnier. Sales of Campari itself continue to rocket and it can be found in 190 countries. Brazil is the biggest market although I'm told that Saint Lucia boasts the highest per capita consumption where – of all things – they like best to mix it with condensed milk. Hmm…

In Milan, the aperitivo is a veritable institution where you hang out with friends, have bits to eat (not too much to spoil dinner) and have a few drinks (not too many to get drunk). You might have an Americano (Campari, red vermouth and soda water), created in Gaspare's own bar; a Sbagliato or 'mistaken' Negroni (Campari, prosecco and red vermouth), first served in Bar Basso; a Garibaldi (Campari and orange juice). Or you might just have a Campari and soda. After all, the evening is ahead of you and there's no need to rush.

25% vol; www.campari.com

CHAIRMAN'S RESERVE RUM, THE FORGOTTEN CASKS SAINT LUCIA

A few years ago, Mrs Ray and I spent a very entertaining few days in Saint Lucia. We stayed at East Winds Inn, one of those stockade-like all-inclusive joints which meant that we ate and – more particularly – drank far more than was good for us. Indeed, Marina took quite a shine to the cocktails that EWI's irritatingly good-looking barman, Titus, created. It's fair to say that she took something of a shine to Titus himself and it was only to remove her from his clutches that we abandoned the confines of our hotel more often than I'd intended.

We filled our time by climbing to the top of Pigeon Island; visiting the towering Pitons; pottering around Anse La Raye (where a spaced-out fisherman offered us the biggest spliff we'd ever seen: 'All home-grown, man, it'll blow your head') and hiring a couple of horses from two hilarious dread-wearing Rastafarian guides and galloping along Cas-en-Bas beach before plunging into the sea to swim with our mounts.

The highlight, though, was our visit to Saint Lucia Distillers, which is where I first met the scrumptious rum that is Chairman's Reserve. After a brief tour, we were encouraged to kick back, relax and sample the whole range. We were also positively discouraged from spitting anything out. 'It's not the Mother's Union here, man!' We tried the Chairman's Reserve white rum, the Original, the spiced rum and then this beauty, The Forgotten Casks, based on the casks of rum hidden and forgotten about after a terrible fire at the distillery in 2007. It's a tongue-teasingly fine, limited-release blend of pot still and Coffey still rums, matured for between six and 11 years in former bourbon casks, and thus too old to be included in Chairman's Reserve Original.

This is sipping rum at its best, full of candied orange, toffee, raisins and exotic fruit. I love it. Mrs Ray loves it too – and hurried back to East Winds Inn to tell Titus all about it.

40% vol; www.chairmansreserverum.com

CHAMBORD FRANCE

Please don't be put off by the outrageously naff-looking bottle which, supposedly based on a regal orb, looks more like something that you would find in a five-year-old's dressing up box rather than among the crown jewels of any self-respecting monarch. Look past the container to what's inside, which is a really rather glorious black raspberry liqueur.

Currently owned by drinks conglomerate, Brown-Forman, Chambord is said to be based on the recipe for an ancient fruit liqueur that was served to French monarchs during the seventeenth century. This may or may not be so. What we do know is that what's marketed and sold today as Chambord – named after the striking Château de Chambord of course – was launched in 1982 and is extremely drinkable.

Produced at Château de la Sistière in the Loire Valley, not far from mighty Chambord itself, the liqueur is based on the finest raspberries and black raspberries (not blackberries, which are different, apparently). The fruits are macerated in neutral spirit for up to a month after which more spirit is added to refresh the mix, which sits for another two weeks. The fruit is then pressed to provide the base of the liqueur, which is then married to a blend of XO cognac, vanilla, citrus peel and honey. A bit of sugar and water are added and the liquid is then filtered and bottled.

I think it's daftly delicious. Nothing artificial is added during production and it just shouts of naturally fresh, rich, ripe berries. Drink it on its own well chilled, pour it over fruit puddings or use it in cocktails such as the Bramble (25ml/ 1fl oz Chambord, 25ml/1fl oz gin, 20ml/4 tsp fresh lemon juice stirred over crushed ice) or the Chambord Martini (25ml/1fl oz Chambord, 25ml/1fl oz vodka, 2 raspberries, 2 blackberries, 2 blueberries, all crushed and shaken together over ice and then strained into a martini glass). My favourite way of drinking Chambord, though, is as a Kir Royal where you simply use Chambord instead of crème de cassis.

16.5% vol; www.chambordchannel.com

43

CHIVAS REGAL 18 GOLD SIGNATURE BLENDED SCOTCH WHISKY SCOTLAND

Chivas Brothers have a 200-year-old history of blending whisky, and aficionados always give them the thumbs up. They make exceptional drams and in Colin Scott, they've a genius at the helm: the Master Blender for over 30 years.

This 18 Year Old is a cracker and if you've already tried it you won't be surprised when I tell you that it won Best Blended Scotch at the 2015 International Whisky Competition and the Blended Scotch Whisky Trophy at the 2014 International Wine & Spirits Competition. We're talking quality here.

Blended whisky sometimes gets looked down upon by those hypnotized by the aura and mystique that surround fine single malt whiskies. Many folk trade up from a simple blend to a fine single malt and leave it at that. Canny folk, though, know that a whisky such as Chivas 18 is just as fine as any top single malt. As Colin Scott once explained to me, single malts might be sexy and easy to understand but a blend will be comprised of said malts and should have complexity and style in buckets. 'It's like going to a party with lots of people rather than just having a conversation with just one person,' he said.

There are over 20 grain and malt whiskies in the Chivas Regal 18 Year Old blend, with malts from Strathisla, the oldest working distillery in Scotland (Est: 1786), at its heart. It's rich, fruity and full-flavoured, velvety smooth and mellow with hints of dark chocolate and heather honey on the finish. They say that even one drop of dew from a rose petal can change the flavour of a dram of whisky and Colin Scott likes to drink his Chivas 18 half-and-half with water, thus allowing the wonderfully complex aromas and flavours to flood out.

Whisky is all about pleasure, not pain, and a whisky such as this should be drunk with a smile on your face, not a grimace, so add water, sit back and sigh with pleasure.

40% vol; www.chivas.com

CLÉMENT CRÉOLE SHRUBB LIQUEUR D'ORANGE MARTINIQUE

I only stumbled upon this recently and, goodness, I'm glad that I did for it's stunning. I love orange-flavoured spirits and liqueurs: they work so well on their own after a meal and are brilliant in cocktails. Cointreau (page 46) and Grand Marnier (page 76) are fond favourites, of course. They're both so different from each other in terms of production, as you know, but a seductive orange-ness is their common link. This Clément Créole, too, has that delightful citrus touch.

It comes from Martinique, a *département d'outre mer* of France, in the eastern Caribbean, and is produced from rhum agricole; i.e. the base spirit – the rum – is distilled from fermented sugar juice rather than molasses and, being French, it's made to strict *appellation contrôlée* regulations.

The distillery of Héritiers H. Clément – the leading producer of Martinique rhum agricole – has been making fine spirits in the town of Le Francois since 1887. Sugar cane from within strictly regulated areas is harvested between March and May and crushed within an hour of being cut. The free-run juice is then fermented in open-top tanks before being distilled in a single column still. The resulting spirit is then either rested in steel tanks for white rum or aged in oak barrels for dark rum.

This is a blend of both white and dark, mixed with Caribbean spices and the peel of bitter oranges. I've got a glass in front of me now and what I love about it is the way the orange notes simply flood out to greet you. They invite you in but don't overwhelm you once you enter. It's not all about orange, though, for there's a backbone of rum too and hints of spice and vanilla. It's oily and creamy on the palate but far from cloying; it's sweet and spicy, with a hint of – maybe – ginger in the background, followed by a fresh finish. It's teasingly, tastily complex but all that it really demands of you is that you take a second glass.

40% vol; www.rhum-clement.com

45

COINTREAU BLOOD ORANGE FRANCE

Cointreau is to triple sec as Hoover is to vacuum cleaners. The specific brand name has become the generic name by which this delicious style of orange liqueur is known.

But although Cointreau is the most celebrated, it wasn't the first. That honour goes to Jean-Baptiste Combier's scrumptiously orangey, triple-distilled liqueur which he invented in the 1830s in Saumur in the Loire, many years before brothers Adolphe and Edouard-Jean Cointreau came up with their distillation of sweet and bitter orange peels in 1849, just down the road in Angers.

Be that as it may, Cointreau is excellent stuff, the inevitable stalwart of such classic cocktails as the White Lady (gin, triple sec and lemon juice); the Margarita (tequila, triple sec and lime juice); the Sidecar (cognac, triple sec and lemon juice); the Kamikaze (vodka and triple sec); the Long Island Iced Tea (vodka, tequila, gin, rum and triple sec) and the Cosmpolitan (vodka, triple sec and cranberry juice), to name just the obvious ones. There are probably at least another 350.

It's said that Cointreau sells around 13 million bottles of their triple sec every year. There's the regular Cointreau, the Cointreau Noir (a blend of triple sec and cognac) and then this, the Cointreau Blood Orange, which I consider to be the star of the range.

A twist on the original Cointreau, aromatic Corsican blood oranges are added to the signature sweet and bitter oranges, the peels of which are distilled together to give a zesty, mouth-filling treat. It's richer, deeper and more satisfying than simple Cointreau and I reckon it's best enjoyed on its own over ice at the end of a meal or turned into a so-called Cointreau Rouge by mixing it half-and-half with cranberry juice and serving over ice in a large wine glass. Yum!

40% vol; www.cointreau.com

COPPER RIVET DOCKYARD GIN ENGLAND

Pretty much anything and everything that comes from Kent gets my vote. It's the Garden of England after all and full of outstanding natural produce. It's a special place. The High Weald and the Kent Downs are as pretty as anywhere in the country and if the White Cliffs of Dover, Leeds Castle (said to be the prettiest in all the world) or Canterbury Cathedral don't stir the heart, there's something seriously wrong with you. The folk who live and work in Kent are special too. After all, unlike the rest of the country, their forebears were – famously – never conquered by William the Bastard in 1066. The county's proud motto – 'Invicta', meaning unvanquished – commemorates this fact. They're a stubborn bunch.

One of Kent's most historic sites is Chatham Dockyard. It was here that Nelson's flagship, HMS Victory, was launched in 1765 and where the Resolute Desk – at which successive presidents of the United States have sat and worked in the Oval Office – was fashioned from the timbers of HMS Resolute in 1880. Of much greater interest to us old soaks though is the fact that Chatham Dockyard's Pump House No. 5 – built in 1873 to drain the docks – became home to the excellent Copper Rivet craft distillery in 2016. Owned and run by Bob Russell and sons Matthew and Stephen, the distillery makes first-rate spirits such as Vela Vodka; Son of a Gun Cask Finished English Grain Spirit and this Dockyard Gin, a superb, small-batch take on traditional naval gins.

Only Kent chalk water and local wheat, barley and rye are used at Copper Rivet and they control the whole process of distillation from grain to glass. They mill the grain and brew and ferment on site before distilling in their handmade copper still. Nine botanicals transform this neutral grain spirit into gin, namely juniper, coriander seeds, grains of paradise, elderflower, lemon peel, orris root, orange peel, angelica and green cardamom. The result is a resoundingly fresh, citrusy and floral gin of star quality and I wouldn't expect anything less from the glory that is Kent.

41.2% vol; www.copperrivetdistillery.com

COURVOISIER 21 YEAR OLD COGNAC
FRANCE

My late father had a theory. He reckoned the main difference between a Frenchman and a Briton was that a Frenchman would wash his hands before going for a pee and a Brit would wash his hands after going for a pee. My pa would invite his listeners (usually just me and I'd heard it many times before) to draw their own conclusions.

He could have pointed out that the French drink more Scotch than the British and that the British drink more cognac than the French. Unlike my old man's rather curious observation (after all, how would he know?) this is a cast-iron fact.

Cognac is famously dominated by four big names – Courvoisier, Hennessy, Martell and Rémy Martin – who between them produce about 80 per cent of the region's brandy. It's Courvoisier, founded in 1809 and now owned by Beam Suntory, which sells by far the most in the UK. For some reason it also seems to attract the most stick. Unfairly so, I reckon. Ok, so its entry-level VS (Very Special) might not in truth be very special at all, at least not compared to Hennessy's, say, but at the other end of the range, the Courvoisier Initiale Extra really is exquisite, full of complex vanilla, cocoa and spicy flavours and this, the Courvoisier 21 Year Old, is a right bobby dazzler too.

This is the first cognac from any of the top houses to be defined by an age statement – much in the manner of a serious single malt whisky – instead of the more usual and confusing VSOP (Very Superior Old Pale), XO (Extra Old) and so on. It's ground-breaking stuff. It's also mouth-fillingly tasty, with nuts, dried fruits and leather on the nose, leading to generous flavours of gingerbread, marzipan, candied orange peel, honey and spice on the palate. The first of its kind, it's a glorious cognac to get stuck into and to be savoured.

40% vol; www.courvoisier.com

CRAIGELLACHIE 23 YEAR OLD SINGLE MALT SCOTCH WHISKY SCOTLAND

If you've been to Speyside, you will doubtless have stayed in or visited the celebrated Craigellachie Hotel. And if you've stayed in or visited the celebrated Craigellachie Hotel you will have spent time in the hotel's fabled Quaich Bar. And if you've spent time in the hotel's fabled Quaich Bar you will undoubtedly have had a dram or so of Craigellachie itself, just one of almost 1,000 whiskies that this wonderful watering hole stocks and serves.

The Craigellachie Distillery is slap-dab next door to the hotel. Founded in 1891 by Peter Mackie, Alexander Edward and a consortium of whisky blenders and brokers, the distillery is now owned by John Dewar & Sons, a subsidiary of Bacardi Ltd. Most of the distillery's output goes into Dewar's White Label, the best-selling blended Scotch whisky in the US, but occasionally part of it is set aside for release as a special bottling and I can't think of a more special bottling than this, the 23 Year Old.

Craigellachie's whiskies age extremely well (they also market a 33 Year Old) and they're noted for their so-called 'muscularity' and weight, due, I gather, to the fact that the distillery uses malted barley from one particular oil-fired kiln in Glenesk and continues to cool its spirit in worm tubs rather than the modern condensers everyone else uses.

Look, the 23 Year Old is pricey, yes, but it really is exceptional, full of spicy, exotic ripe fruit, citrus and vanilla and goodness knows what else. Try it neat first and then add water and see how the flavours envelop you. And if, like me, you would struggle to spend nigh on four hundred quid for a bottle (over $500), then do as I did and simply sit by the fire in the Quaich and have a wee dram of it for £29 ($40).

46% vol; www.craigellachie.com

HOW SPIRITS ARE MADE

Ok, this is a book about spirits and liqueurs so I'd better explain, very briefly, what such things are. Boring but crucial. A spirit is any unsweetened alcoholic drink of 20% vol or above that has been produced by distilling the fermented liquid of pretty much any raw material that contains starch, such as cereals, potatoes, sugar cane, grapes and even – good grief – tapioca (see page 92).

Whisky, for example, is made by grinding or 'milling' malted barley (that's barley that has been soaked in water and warmed to encourage germination, turning starch to sugar) into grist and putting it into a mash tun with hot water. The resulting sweet liquid, or 'wort', is cooled and put into a large wooden vessel called a washback, along with some yeast. This ferments, giving a liquid of about 8% vol called 'wash'. This is piped into a copper wash still and heated so as to boil off the alcohol. The vapour rises into the neck of the still and then down a water-cooled condenser, returning to liquid form known as 'low wines', at around 25% vol. The low wines are piped into the spirit still and heated again. As the liquid falls through the condenser, the heart, or 'middle cut', of the spirit is retained at somewhere between 66% and 72% vol. This goes into the collecting tank and thence into the cask for ageing.

The length of fermentation, speed of distillation and the shape of the still all affect a whisky's ultimate flavour. Arguably, the key element, though, is the oak the whisky ages in. Casks (they're seldom called barrels in Scotland) which have previously held either bourbon or oloroso sherry are most commonly used. The size and age of the casks, the source and type of the oak, and the location and type of the warehouse the casks are matured in all add to the final whisky's nuances of expression.

Brandy is made from distilling fermented grape juice better known as, erm, wine. Rum is distilled either from fermented sugar cane juice or from molasses. Vodka is distilled from anything from barley to potatoes to sugar beet to grapes. Gin is simply redistilled or 'rectified' vodka with added flavours (chiefly juniper) and so on.

And a liqueur is simply a spirit that has been sweetened and flavoured with anything from herbs to spices to fruits to cream. Such drinks can be as low as 15% vol and go up to, well – in the case of the Élixir Végétal de la Grande-Chartreuse – as high as 69% vol.

Vermouth is simply an aromatized wine and is neither a spirit nor a liqueur but I mention it here since several examples are included in this book. After all, how the heck could you have a Dry Martini, Manhattan, Negroni or Vesper without a splash of vermouth?

"A PERFECT MARTINI SHOULD BE MADE BY FILLING A GLASS WITH GIN, THEN WAVING IT IN THE GENERAL DIRECTION OF ITALY."

NOËL COWARD

DARROZE LES GRANDS ASSEMBLAGES 12 YEAR OLD ARMAGNAC FRANCE

They serve a delicious cocktail in the Connaught Bar at The Connaught hotel in London called Sting Like a Bee, created by the bar's resident mixology genius, Agostino Perrone. At £19 ($25) a pop I can only ever afford to have just the one but it does tee one up very nicely for whatever lies ahead. A mix of bee pollen-infused Darroze Armagnac, champagne, orange blossom syrup and lime juice, it's giggle-makingly delicious and shows just how great a cocktail ingredient armagnac can be.

Of course, Darroze is a name that's familiar to habitués of The Connaught, for Hélène of that ilk is the hotel's much-lauded Michelin-starred chef and it's her brother Marc who produces the exceptional brandies that bear the family name.

Marc took over from his father Francis in 1996, having learned from him the skills needed to rootle out undiscovered and little-known producers in Bas Armagnac. He works with around 30 individual estates and ages their armagnacs in his cellars, releasing them as part of his Unique Collection.

Alongside this project, Marc has also come up with his own range of blends called Les Grands Assemblages, aged for eight, 12, 20, 30, 40, 50 and 60 years, the stated age being that of the youngest armagnac in the blend. It's an impressive and deeply authentic selection for sure and despite the merits and delights of the older ones, I still plump for this, the 12 Year Old. That's to say that I don't think that the 30 Year Old is over £80 ($100) better than this, which is deliciously spicy, fruity and lively and certainly grand enough for me.

On the other hand, I notice that you can get a magnum of 12 Year Old for just £120 ($160), which also seems a bargain. Imagine uncorking that at home. What a tiptoptastic party that would be!

43% vol; www.darroze-armagnacs.com

DELAMAIN PALE & DRY XO GRANDE CHAMPAGNE COGNAC FRANCE

Delamain & Co have been making cognacs in the town of Jarnac since 1759 and the company (which wasn't officially founded until 1824) remains family-owned. They only produce cognacs of XO quality and above and their signature cognac, the fabled Pale & Dry, is a blend of 25-year-old eaux-de-vie drawn exclusively from the finest Grande Champagne vineyards. Each part of the blend is aged separately in well-seasoned Limousin oak casks before being brought together, 'married' for two years, and then bottled.

The light, pale (no colouring is added) and elegantly floral and fruity cognac (nor is any sugar) has power and persistence and is just so stylish. It's a delight to drink and should be where a fine evening starts rather than ends.

My dear old dad loved cognac (he wrote a definitive book on the subject) and although he was deeply fond of the cognacs of Camus, this beauty was his absolute favourite and it was a rare evening that I didn't see him enjoying a large glass of it. I love it too and always think of him when I drink it. Pa was an inveterate limerick writer and nothing fuelled his inspiration better than these post-prandial beakers of Delamain. He penned these lines after a jolly evening we spent together:

I do like a nice glass of brandy –
It makes me feel dashing and dandy,
(And sucks-boo to those
Who chose to suppose
I'd be bound to rhyme 'brandy' with 'randy'...)

It's not quite the same thing with whisky
Which is well known for making you frisky,
But in Sauchiehall Street,
Where they take the stuff neat,
To be frisky on whisky is risky...

40% vol; www.delamain-cognac.fr

53

DERRUMBES OAXACA JOVEN MEZCAL
MEXICO

My good chum Mike, recently returned from Mexico City, tells me that anyone who is anyone takes mezcal to parties these days rather than tequila, which is now deemed a bit old hat in some quarters. Mezcal is enjoying huge popularity both over there and over here and Mike, whose favourite tipple hitherto has been Tuaca (page 144), developed such a taste for it on his travels that he's keenly been pursuing his researches back in Blighty with me as his willing assistant.

Our local and very fine Mexican restaurant – Carlito Burrito in Brighton's York Place – boasts 15 different mezcals on its list (compared to just eight tequilas by the way) and this from the Central Valley of Oaxaca in southwest Mexico is by some margin our favourite.

Made using espadín and wild tobalá agave that has been cooked in an underground pit over black oak, then pressed and fermented in pine wood vats and double distilled in copper pot stills before resting for three months in large glass bottles, it's extraordinarily complex. There are hints of honey, citrus, spice, wood smoke and, hmmm, maybe nail polish or such like on the nose and sweet cooked fruit, citrus, herbs and pine on the palate. It has an exceptionally profound character and speaks of the earth it comes from in a way that not too many spirits do. It's a true craft spirit made by the small artisan.

Mike and I knock it back with relish in Carlito Burrito in our very English way although I'm told that in Mexico it's not unusual to enjoy it with sliced citrus fruit covered in sprinklings of ground, fried larva, chilli pepper and something I'm not overly keen in getting to know well: worm salt.

Mike says it's absolutely delicious and definitely the done thing. But then, as I say, Mike's a fan of Tuaca…

48% vol; www.mezcalderrumbes.mx

DIDIER LEMORTON RÉSERVE DOMFRONTAIS CALVADOS FRANCE

Last year my wife, boys and I had a very cheery couple of weeks pottering about Normandy and Brittany. We visited Bayeux, Caen, Rennes, Josselin with its imposing castle and Vannes with its pretty bridge and Vieux Port. On the way back we even made it to Le Mans and discovered that it's not all about motorsport. There's a charming old town that's definitely worth a stare and a striking sixth-century cathedral (well, it was started in the sixth century but finished in the fourteenth), the stained-glass windows of which alone make it worth the visit.

We ate and drank like kings and there wasn't a day that went past when the boys didn't have a crêpe or a Tarte Normande and Marina and I didn't have a bucket of cider and pretty much the same of calvados. My only sadness was that, although we passed tantalizingly close by, we didn't pop into the village of Mantilly to shake the hand and pat the back of Didier Lemorton, the wizard behind this astonishingly fine calvados. We knocked back an awful lot of it during our jaunt and it never failed to bring a smile to our lips.

The Lemorton domaine comprises 100 hectares of orchards with 40 different varieties of apples and – crucially – pears. Unlike the rest of Calvados, here in the southern part of the region, the so-called Domfrontais, the *appellation contrôlée* laws require producers to include a minimum of 30 per cent pears alongside the apples. Lemorton uses 70 per cent.

He ages his cider for a year in oak before distillation in an alembic still. The spirit must then be aged in oak for a minimum three years whereas Lemorton ages his for five (elsewhere in Calvados it's two). This ageing gives depth and character and a touch of vanilla sweetness; the high preponderance of pears gives lightness and elegance. If you know of a better calvados, pray lead me to it.

40% vol; www.lemorton.com

DOLIN DE CHAMBÉRY DRY WHITE VERMOUTH FRANCE

The Dry Martini, ah, the Dry Martini, now there's a drink. And are there any drinks more eulogized or mythologized?

As any fule kno – or at least as any fan of the *Thin Man* films kno – the important thing when shaking a Dry Martini is the rhythm. You should always have rhythm in your shaking. The perfect Dry Martini is, of course, shaken to waltz time whereas a Manhattan is shaken to foxtrot time and a Bronx to two-step time. Do keep up.

It was my father who introduced me to the *Thin Man* series (1934–47) when in my late teens and I've been an addict ever since. If you don't know them, do watch them. They might be dated but, crikey, they're funny and so deliciously politically incorrect.

It was my pa, too, of course, who introduced me to the delights of the Dry Martini. He liked them dry but not as dry as – I think it was – film director Luis Buñuel who would pour ice-cold gin into a frozen glass and then pass an unopened bottle of vermouth in front of the glass through a shaft of sunlight. Now that was dry.

No, my father liked his with a decent hint of vermouth and the only vermouth he considered was Dolin, founded in 1815 or 1821 – depending on whom in the company you believe – and recognized as the inventor of Vermouth de Chambéry in Savoie.

Dolin make their vermouth by macerating scores of local plants and herbs in white base wine and by adding a bit of sugar. It's the lightest of all the finest vermouths and I love that about it. It's almost watery white in the glass and so light on the palate, so fresh, so aromatic, so delicate. It's great on its own as an easy-going, early evening, pick-me-up but even better with a kick of gin or vodka.

As Nick Charles, hero of the aforementioned films, says to his son when he senses a Dry Martini might be in the offing: 'Nicky, something tells me that something important is happening somewhere and I think we should be there.'

Me too.

17.5% vol; www.dolin.fr

"WHY DON'T YOU SLIP OUT OF THOSE WET CLOTHES AND INTO A DRY MARTINI?"

ROBERT BENCHLEY

DRAMBUIE SCOTLAND

Have you ever had a Heather Martini? No? Well, for heaven's sake proceed with caution. I had a couple of glasses of it only the other evening at a belated Burns Night with our neighbours. It was gloriously tasty but savagely alcoholic too and folk were up dancing on the tables before the haggis had even been caught, plucked, prepared and put in the oven or I'd managed to polish my small talk.

A Heather Martini is blessedly simple to make (and to drink) and boasts just three, all-Scottish ingredients. Shake 50ml (1¾fl oz) of Caorunn gin, 20ml (4 tsp) of Drambuie and 5ml (1 tsp) of Talisker 10 Year Old Single Malt over ice and strain into a cocktail glass. If anything will put some Ross into your Cromarty, this will.

Its most distinctive ingredient, Drambuie, is as Scottish as they come of course. The legend goes that when Bonnie Prince Charlie fled to the Isle of Skye after defeat at the Battle of Culloden in 1746, he was given refuge by the Clan MacKinnon. It's said that he repaid his hosts with the secret recipe to this, his own private liqueur. The recipe got passed here and there over the following centuries until it ended up, in 2014, with William Grant & Sons, owners of Glenfiddich amongst other well-known distilleries.

The original recipe called for a brandy base whereas Drambuie is now famously based on a blend of grain whiskies, Speyside and Highland malt whiskies aged up to 15 years, and a mix of heather honey, herbs and spices.

I don't often drink it but when I do I always wonder why not. It's ridiculously moreish either on its own over ice or as part of a Rusty Nail, that cocktail so beloved of Frank Sinatra's Rat Pack which calls for one measure of Drambuie and two of fine Scotch whisky to be stirred over ice in an Old Fashioned glass and served with a twist of lemon. It's even simpler than a Heather Martini to make although the effect of it is nigh on identical.

40% vol; www.drambuie.com

EL DORADO 15 YEAR OLD SPECIAL RESERVE RUM GUYANA

If you only ever drink one rum in your life, make sure it's this one. An astoundingly fine cask-aged rum from Guyana, it has won the trophy for Best Rum in the World at the International Wine & Spirit Competition an unparalleled six times and against some pretty stout-hearted competition at that. It's a double-funnelled, twin-screwed, ocean-going belter.

Technically, rum is any spirit made from sugar cane and its derivatives using either a pot still or a column still (or both) and is produced all along the Equator and pretty much wherever sugar cane is grown. The rum made in and around the Caribbean, though, is the best and most prized. Rum made in French-influenced Caribbean islands is known as rhum agricole, and is distilled from sugar cane juice; rum made in British-influenced islands (or, in this case, territories, given that Guyana is on the South American mainland) is what the British call rum and the French sometimes call rhum industriel and is distilled from molasses, a by-product of sugar production.

This, produced at the Diamond Distillery (the last distillery in Guyana) on the east bank of the Demerara River is one of the latter rums and one so fine as to hold its head up alongside the most complex cognacs, armagnacs and single malts. And as with single malts, the age statement on the label refers only to the youngest spirits in the blend so, although it contains several rums that are almost 25 years old, since the youngest are 15 years old, that's what the label must say.

A blend of distillates from four separate stills (both column and pot), aged separately in old bourbon casks, blended and then left in cask again to marry, it's astonishingly smooth, with oodles of sweetness and spice, hints of ginger, prunes, honey and a gratifyingly long, almost chocolately finish. You will love it. And if you don't, then I'm afraid you're lost to me forever.

43% vol; www.theeldoradorum.com

ELIJAH CRAIG SMALL BATCH BOURBON
USA

Kentucky is known for the Three Big Sins – tobacco, racing and bourbon – and there are few nicer places to get led astray than the Bluegrass State.

I invariably base myself at the Seelbach Hotel in Louisville, and a magnificent old pile it is too, famous for having been one of Al Capone's haunts. If you ask nicely, someone will show you the room in which Scarface played cards and from where he fled the cops via a secret passage.

They do a sumptuous Sunday brunch in the Oakroom at the Seelbach, ideal for restoring equilibrium after a day on the Mint Juleps at Churchill Downs and a night on the bourbon in Louisville. I know you won't believe me, but when I was last there I had – on one massive plate – duck prosciutto, cassoulet, baked ham, asparagus, fried eggs, grilled tomatoes, roast Brussels sprouts and beef Wellington. Oh, and a bacon burger. Just a small one.

The hotel also boasts the excellent Old Seelbach Bar, and it was here on my first ever visit to Kentucky that I had my first ever bourbon in situ, so to speak. Dazzled by the extraordinary selection on the back bar, I dithered, asking simply for a bourbon on the rocks and this is what I got. Actually, to be strictly accurate, the barman poured me some Elijah Craig 12 Year Old, but, owing to pressure on stocks, they no longer make that, this being its extremely tasty replacement.

The Rev Elijah Craig was a preacher and a distiller, credited with being the first to mature his whiskey in charred oak barrels, and the whiskey that bears his name is produced by the Heaven Hill Distillery Company. The Elijah Craig Small Batch has no age statement but is comprised of whiskeys between eight and twelve years old and it's extremely fine, festooned with awards since its launch in 2016.

Smooth, mellow, sweet and slightly smoky, slightly spicy, it's great sipped on its own on the rocks, although I'm not sure I don't like it best in an Old Fashioned. Or a Mint Julep. Or a Boulevardier. Or a…

47% vol; www.elijahcraig.com

"CANDY IS DANDY, BUT LIQUOR IS QUICKER."

OGDEN NASH, *HARD LINES*

FOUR ROSES SMALL BATCH BOURBON
USA

For many, Four Roses is synonymous with bourbon. It's one of the most popular brands of all, one of the best – and one of the best-priced. Indeed, it was *Whisky Magazine*'s American Whiskey Distiller of the year in 2011, 2012 and 2013.

To be called bourbon, a whiskey has to be made in the United States (almost all of it comes from Kentucky), from a minimum of 51 per cent corn spirit, bottled at 40% vol or more with no addition of either colour or flavour. And only charred, virgin oak barrels may be used in its maturation. This last stipulation is thanks to the late Wilbur D. Mills, Democratic Congressman for Arkansas, who helped draft the 1935 Federal Alcohol Administration Act, in which the methods by which bourbon should be made were set down.

Lobbied by canny timber barons of his home state, Mills ensured that bourbon was required to be matured in brand new barrels made from American white oak, the largest supply of which is in the great Ozark forests of Arkansas. Said barrels had to be charred, following a practice attributed to Elijah Craig (see page 60), an eighteenth-century preacher and distiller, who found the best way to prepare an old fish barrel for storing whiskey was to set fire to its inside. After a single use, the barrels are mostly sold to Scottish distilleries.

Famously smooth, Four Roses Small Batch is spicy, toasty, honeyed, fruity and full of toffee and vanilla. As for Wilbur Mills, well, it all went a bit pear-shaped. He's now best remembered for the outrage he caused in the 1970s, running around with a stripper called Fanne Foxe (aka 'The Argentine Firecracker') and for being arrested by the police in Washington DC, drunk as a skunk behind the wheel of his car, blood dripping from scratches to his face courtesy of Miss Foxe, who promptly hurled herself into the Tidal Basin. She survived; his career didn't.

45% vol; www.fourrosesbourbon.com

FOURSQUARE SPICED RUM BARBADOS

I'm not usually a fan of spiced rum but I'm a huge fan of this. All too often spiced rum is sweet and sickly and does nothing to enhance the image of fine rum and does nothing to promote a feeling of wellbeing in the drinker either. They are sometimes little better than alcopops and you can't help feeling that the spices they've lobbed in are simply there to mask the poor quality of the distillate, which is often just low-grade white rum with added caramel colouring. I think you know which ones I'm talking about.

Foursquare Spiced Rum is as fine an example as you will find anywhere. I drank no end of it last year pottering about Barbados whilst island-hopping in the Caribbean. Oh don't be like that, I was working. Besides, just getting between the islands is a job of work in itself, as anyone will tell you, given that local airline LIAT (the Leeward Islands Air Transport) is known to its long-suffering passengers as either Leaving Island Any Time or Luggage In Any Terminal.

Anyway, I've stopped being cross now, the bags finally turned up, and I digress. The Foursquare Distillery in St Philip in the south of the island is housed in a derelict former sugar factory dating from the mid seventeenth century and is owned by the Seale family, of whom the famously quality-focused Richard Seale represents the fifth generation.

And some spectacular cask-aged rums are made here. If you've never tried Doorly's 12 Year Old, for example, you're in for a treat. But I bet you love this spiced rum as much as I do too, a blend of pot and column stills, aged for at least two years and without a hint of any nasty addition of colouring.

It's spicy for sure, but it's easy on the vanilla and more focused on cloves, candied orange and even ginger. Don't waste it in cocktails; sup it neat over ice whilst waiting for your luggage to turn up.

37.5% vol; www.rumsixtysix.com

I've always had a soft spot for the gins of Foxdenton Estate, owned and run by the ever ebullient Nick Radclyffe. The Foxdenton Original 48 London Dry Gin is mighty fine and one of the best there is for making a Negroni. It's smooth and aromatic with a creamy texture and, at 48% vol, is punchier than most gins, giving the Negroni even more of a fearsome kick.

Do you remember those signs that you used to see in the windows of small French restaurants that declared 'Le patron mange ici'? There was one such establishment in Wardour Street, Soho, where I often spied the genial proprietor at a window table tucking into some blanquette de veau or coq au vin, napkin tucked into his shirt, bottle of red almost empty. Nick Radclyffe is cut from the very same cloth and declares proudly: 'We only make what we enjoy drinking ourselves.'

Well, what the Radclyffes clearly enjoy drinking is fruit gin. Foxdenton Estate boasts a formidable array and so darn tasty are they that the punters lap them up – well, they lap up whatever the Radclyffes are kind enough to leave them – and these gins now far outsell the Original 48.

The range includes: Rhubarb Gin, Raspberry Gin, Golden Apricot Gin, Damson Gin, Sloe Gin, Lemon and Cucumber Gin, Christmas Liqueur and the superbly named Martha's Marvellous Jumping Juice, created in league with Martha,

Lady Sitwell, as the perfect stirrup cup for those foolhardy enough to head out on a horse for a day's hurtling over hedges and fences.

My favourite, though, is the Winslow Plum Gin made from Opal, Victoria and Jubilee plums picked in Buckinghamshire, Herefordshire and Shropshire. When added to a glass of fizz it makes a perfect 11A.M. reviver and when drunk neat or on the rocks, a sublime after-dinner treat.

You can buy it in 5cl minis (ideal for leaving on your guests' bedside tables as a night cap), normal bottles or in the spectacular, one-gallon 'Goliath', which is what I call a true statement of intent and tells me all I need to know about the Radclyffes' drinking habits.

17.5% vol; www.foxdentonestate.co.uk

"WHEN I READ ABOUT THE EVILS OF DRINKING, I GAVE UP READING."

HENNY YOUNGMAN

FRAPIN MILLÉSIME 1988 XO COGNAC
FRANCE

It always baffles me that the extraordinary cognacs of Maison Frapin aren't better known. I mean, they're beloved in the trade by merchants, mixologists, sommeliers and restaurateurs, of course, it's just that they don't seem to have the wider fame that they deserve.

Those that know them, adore them. There was a famous dinner many years ago at which HM the Q was entertained at 10 Downing Street by her then five surviving prime ministers: Tony Blair, Sir John Major, Lady Thatcher, Lord Callaghan and Sir Edward Heath.

As you might imagine, they dined pretty darn well (on cured duck breast, roast turbot and raspberry cranachan, I think it was) and drank well too, knocking back the likes of a 1995 JJ Prüm Wehlener Sonnenuhr Riesling Spätlese, 1962 Château Latour, 1985 Pol Roger and 1955 Taylor's Port. Finally, with coffee, they had a 1948 Frapin Château Fontpinot Cognac no less. I only mention this to show the sort of bottles that Frapin rubs shoulders with and the sort of company it keeps.

But please don't let such politicos' fondness for it put you off, for this 1988 successor to the mighty 1948 is a strikingly fine cognac. One of the treasures from Frapin's private reserves, it's produced from only those grapes grown in the vineyard that surrounds Château Fontpinot, the largest single estate in the Grande Champagne region of Cognac.

The Frapin family first settled here in 1270 and have grown grapes and distilled cognac for some 20 generations. The company is currently run by Jean-Pierre Cointreau, a direct descendent of the founder, not to mention a descendent of the creator of Cointreau (see page 46) and founder of Rémy Martin Cognac too.

Only 1,000 bottles of this nectar were made, aged for 25 years in Limousin oak casks at the château. It's deeply flavoured, full of dried and candied fruits with an added hint of vanilla and a rich, almost creamy finish.

It's supremely elegant and nobody else produces cognacs like these. They're rare and exotic for sure (with a price tag to match), but not so rare and exotic that only monarchs or prime ministers can drink them.

41.5% vol; www.cognac-frapin.com

> "IT TAKES ONLY ONE DRINK TO GET ME DRUNK. THE TROUBLE IS, I CAN'T REMEMBER IF IT'S THE THIRTEENTH OR THE FOURTEENTH."
>
> GEORGE BURNS

COGNAC OR ARMAGNAC?

Cognac or armagnac? Hmmm, now there's a question… I love them both and when I'm with one, all thoughts of the other instantly disappear. A bit like claret and burgundy, I suppose, or blondes and brunettes.

Cognac is often likened to silk and armagnac to velvet: the one smooth, poised, elegant and sensual; the other mellow, soft, characterful and earthy. Or as a proud Gascon friend once put it, cognac is the beautiful, refined aristocratic lady you take to the opera; armagnac is the wild Bohemian girl you spend the night with.

Although not far apart geographically (about 150 miles/240 kilometres), the two brandies are indeed very different. They come from different terroirs, enjoy different climates, use different grapes and undergo different methods of distillation: cognac is made by double distillation whereas almost all armagnac is made by the continuous or single distillation process.

Armagnac is France's oldest spirit, having celebrated its official 700th anniversary in 2010. Cognac, though, is the bigger concern, with 80,000 hectares of vineyards compared to armagnac's 3,700 and with annual sales of some 160 million bottles compared to armagnac's 6 million. It's said that each year the wooden casks of cognac lose roughly the same amount through evaporation – the so-called 'Angels' Share' – as a year's production of armagnac.

And where four big firms dominate cognac, armagnac is home to 2,000 or so small artisan producers of whom only around 250 make enough to bottle and sell commercially. Many don't even have their own still.

If you believe their advocates, though, there's one major similarity: they are both effectively health drinks. The great Bernard Hine once adamantly assured me that cognac was good for one because the alcohol doesn't go straight into the bloodstream as it does with an aperitif drunk on an empty stomach, and because it kills the fats from the meal and doesn't make one sleepy.

And as for armagnac, as long ago as the fourteenth century, Cardinal Vital Dufour declared that it 'cures gout, cankers and fistula by ingestion, restores the paralysed member by massage and heals wounds of the skin by application… It enlivens the spirit, recalls the past to memory, renders men joyous, preserves youth and retards senility.'

Well, there must be something in this, because recent studies at Bordeaux University suggest that armagnac helps prevent heart attacks and thrombosis when consumed regularly and in moderation and, despite the amount of animal fat the good people of Gascony eat (think of all that foie gras and confit de canard), the quantity they drink and the number of cigarettes they smoke, they enjoy a lower level of heart disease than anyone else in France, and live an average five years longer.

Come on, I'll drink to that!

"HERE'S TO ALCOHOL, THE ROSE COLOURED GLASSES OF LIFE."

F. SCOTT FITZGERALD, *THE BEAUTIFUL AND DAMNED*

GABRIEL BOUDIER CRÈME DE CASSIS DE DIJON FRANCE

Everyone should have a bottle of crème de cassis in their cupboard or – more properly – in their fridge. And this is the one to have. It is, if you'll forgive the pun, the crème de la crème of crème de cassis.

The House of Gabriel Boudier was founded in Dijon in 1874 and remains family-owned and – goodness! – they make some exquisite crèmes and liqueurs there. If you haven't tried Boudier's crème de myrtilles, crème de pêches or crème de mûres you're in for a treat. Ditto the rhubarb and lychee options. And the Darjeeling tea liqueur is a thing of wonder.

Boudier's finest and most famous product, though, is this beauty, made simply by macerating the finest, ripest blackcurrants in alcohol without any preservatives or colouring agents. Since blackcurrants are so acidic, a small amount of sugar is added and that's it. It's stunning. Even the much-imitated label is gorgeous.

You will, I'm sure, know the story of Canon Félix Kir, the French World War Two resistance fighter who later became mayor of Dijon. Famously, he was in the habit of adding a sweetening dash of crème de cassis to his regular aperitif of the sharp and acidic local Bourgogne Aligoté white wine. This caught on and the drink – the Kir – was named after him.

Less well known is the story behind Boudier's square bottles. There was a glass shortage during World War Two and it was hard to bottle anything at all, let alone crème de cassis. An American general asked the company to make some gin for his officers' mess and Boudier asked to be paid in bottles, which they were – square-shouldered gin bottles. These proved a blessing as they were so distinctive and memorable that sales rocketed. I'm happy to say recipe and bottle remain the same today.

20% vol; www.boudier.com

GLENFARCLAS 21 YEAR OLD SINGLE MALT SCOTCH WHISKY SCOTLAND

If Pol Roger is the house champagne at the *Spectator* – at which magazine I'm lucky enough to be drinks editor – then Glenfarclas is the house spirit. We famously have more bottles of Pol in the office fridge than we do milk...

Glenfarclas is never shy to show its face at 22 Old Queen Street either and we get through buckets of it at the notoriously bibulous *Spectator* summer party where it's drunk neat on the rocks, with ginger ale or in some fancy-dan cocktail. No surprise really, for not only is it bloody good, it's also part of Pol Roger (UK)'s portfolio of family-owned wineries and distilleries where it rubs shoulders with Maison Joseph Drouhin of Burgundy, Domaine Josmeyer of Alsace and Robert Sinskey Vineyards of California.

The distillery was founded in 1856 by John Grant and has been owned and run by the same family ever since. George Grant, the current director of sales, represents the sixth generation. The family relish this independence. As George once told me, 'I get to take the credit for whisky my grandfather made and any mistakes I make won't be noticed until I'm long gone.'

The 10 Year Old is the dram of choice at the *Spectator*, largely due to cost more than anything else. If price were no object, we'd all plump for this gorgeous 21 Year Old which, now I think about it, when compared with the 21-year-old rum and 21-year-old cognac featured elsewhere in these pages, is actually rather a snip at under £90 ($120).
It comes in a dark brown bottle because, owing to the fact that the Grants refuse to use the caramel beloved of many other distilleries, there are sometimes variations in colour. Aged entirely in old oloroso sherry casks, it's rich, rounded and profound. There's candied and tropical fruit, nuts, toffee and spice and the sweet, biscuity finish lasts forever.

43% vol; www.glenfarclas.com

GLENFIDDICH IPA EXPERIMENT SINGLE MALT SCOTCH WHISKY SCOTLAND

Every Scotch whisky distillery has something to boast about and each one is unique in its own way. It tickles me, though, how deep the writers of the various adverts, brochures and press releases dig to highlight this. Old Pulteney, for example, is unique because it's 'the most northerly distillery on the mainland'. The Glenlivet is unique because it was 'the first Highland distillery to be licensed to make Scotch whisky'. Cardhu is unique because it was 'the only malt distillery pioneered by a woman'. Benromach is unique because it's 'the smallest working distillery in Speyside'. Glen Grant is unique because it's 'the only distillery named after its owners'. Dallas Dhu is unique because it was 'the last distillery to be built in the nineteenth century'. Glenfiddich is unique because it's 'the best-selling single malt whisky in the world'. Hang on, you what? Oh, right. That really is something to crow about.

Founded in 1886 by William Grant in the glen of the River Fiddich in Speyside, the distillery is still family-owned and has won more awards for its whiskies than any other Scottish distillery. Oh, sorry, didn't I mention that? I've always enjoyed Glenfiddich's core range. The signature expression, the 12 Year Old, is light, fresh and fragrant. The 15 Year Old Solera Reserve is deliciously honeyed. The 18 Year Old is smooth and creamy and the 21 Year Old Gran Reserva, finished in rum casks, is wonderfully spicy. My current favourite, though, is this, the Glenfiddich IPA Experiment, released in 2017 to whoops of delight from whisky lovers the world over.

A joint collaboration between Glenfiddich and the Speyside Craft Brewery led to the creation of a special India Pale Ale, the casks of which were then used to finish this single malt. The result is spectacular and marks the first time, as far as I'm aware, that a whisky has been thus finished. It's fresh, hoppy, fruity and citrusy and blessed with an underlying sweetness. It was the first release in the Glenfiddich Experimental Series and looks set to join the core range. I say hoorah to that.

43% vol; www.glenfiddich.com

GLENKINCHIE 12 YEAR OLD SINGLE MALT SCOTCH WHISKY SCOTLAND

Dave Broom knows more about whisky than anyone I know. And although he humbly describes himself as simply a Glaswegian who's paid to drink, he's one of the world's leading authorities and has written reams on the subject. What DB doesn't know about whisky ain't worth knowing.

And Dave's a canny fox, too, having devised a so-called Single Malt Whisky Flavour Map (in cahoots with Diageo) to prove his theory that there's a malt whisky for everyone. The grid is dotted with dozens of examples, their co-ordinates determined by how light, smoky, rich and delicate they are.

This little cracker, the Glenkinchie 12 Year Old, is in the bottom left hand quadrant, a mix of light and delicate, and it's the dram that proved to my hitherto whisky-detesting wife, Marina, that she's crazy about the stuff after all. Tired of her antipathy towards his beloved *uisge beatha*, Dave sat Marina down in our local and asked her what drinks she did like. The answer of Earl Grey tea, New Zealand Sauvignon Blanc, old red burgundy and a fine G&T sent him scurrying to the bar. He returned with some Glenkinchie 12 and I'll never forget the slow smile that crept across Marina's chops as she sipped at the glass and how said smile turned into a mouth-splitting grin once she added a little water. 'Oh my goodness!' she declared as she savoured the delicate peach, apricot, vanilla, toffee, unripe banana and cream notes. 'Why has nobody ever told me I liked whisky?' Dave just rolled his eyes.

Glenkinchie 12 is indeed a delight and has since become a staple in our house. The distillery, barely 15 miles from Edinburgh (it's sometimes known as the Edinburgh Malt), is one of just six in the Scottish Lowlands and is noted for the delicacy and elegance of its expressions. When you're next in Edinburgh, make use of the distillery's excellent shuttle bus and discover for yourself just how delicate and elegant.

43% vol; www.malts.com/en-gb/distilleries/glenkinchie/

GLENMORANGIE SIGNET HIGHLAND SINGLE MALT SCOTCH WHISKY SCOTLAND

Every whisky-lover enjoys a dram of Glenmorangie, a distillery well known for the complexity of its whiskies. Indeed, if just one word was used to describe any Glenmo expression, I reckon it would be 'complex'. The whiskies are just so, well, multi-layered and, yes, complex.

The 10 Year Old Original from Glenmorangie has long been my go-to dram of choice. I mean, it's nigh on perfect, being citrusy, honeyed and gently spicy. And, gracious, I love the 18 Year Old too – its lemony freshness, its hint of coconut and its long, sweet finish. Oh, and before I forget, Glenmorangie rhymes with 'orangey' (the colour of the Original's label), as in 'Glen-morangey' rather than with 'Angie' as in 'Glen-more-Angie'. Just saying.

But the dram that takes the biscuit, so to speak, is surely this, the majestic Signet. I first tried it at the distillery itself, which, with its eight towering pot stills – the tallest in all Scotland – is a veritable cathedral to single malt Scotch. Having tried all manner of maturing expressions from various casks, a shot of Signet was wafted under my beak and I was seduced in a trice. It was almost sinfully enticing.

On the nose, the undiluted dram revealed coffee, molasses and orange; on the palate: apricots, butterscotch and coffee again. I added water and got hazelnuts, spice, almonds, vanilla and orange. I added more water and soft citrus notes emerged along with chocolate, coffee, cut grass and straw.

Some of the whiskies used in Signet's creation are almost 40 years old and the end result is sumptuously fine and a worthy winner of Whisky of the Year at the 2016 International Whisky Competition. It's just so – hmmm – what's the word? Oh I know, complex. It's just so darn complex.

46% vol; www.glenmorangie.com

GRAN PATRÓN PLATINUM SILVER TEQUILA
MEXICO

Well, this is grown-up stuff for sure. The first super-premium Blanco tequila, it commands a mighty price which some new to the delights of tequila might jib at. After all, why pay £225 ($300) for a bottle when you could get two bottles of Hine Homage XO Cognac (page 86) for the same price? Because it's special, that's why. Tequila made from 100 per cent blue agave comes in four forms: Blanco/Plata ('white/silver', which is aged for less than two months in steel or oak); Reposado ('rested': aged for a minimum two months and maximum two years in oak); Añejo ('aged/extra aged': aged for a minimum one year and maximum three in oak); and Extra Añejo ('ultra aged': aged for a minimum three years in oak).

Oh, and there's basic Mixto ('mixed') tequila too, which has to be made from at least 51 per cent agave with the remaining 49 per cent made up by anything from sugar cane syrup, to oak flavouring, to caramel and goodness knows what else. If a bottle just says 'Tequila' on the label it'll be the latter and pretty bloody rough. The stuff you and I are after is anything that says 'Tequila 100% de Agave' on it.

Since Blanco has little or no ageing, it shows off tequila in its purest form. It can be the harshest of the expressions but this is anything but. Indeed, it's absurdly smooth. Produced from the finest 100 per cent blue agave with a high sugar content, it's triple distilled and then rested in neutral oak for a month after which whatever colour the spirit picks up is filtered out, leaving it bright and clear as a mountain stream.

This Platinum Silver Tequila comes in a numbered, crystal glass bottle and presentation case and it won't surprise you to learn that its popularity has been driven by club culture. It's beloved of the coolest of cool rappers and blingiest of blingmeisters. Yes, I know it's pricey but if tequila is your thing and you want to rap with the best, this is the one, bro.

40% vol; www.patrontequila.com

GRAND MARNIER CORDON ROUGE LIQUEUR FRANCE

You and I probably first came across Grand Marnier in exactly the same way: as the essential and rather dramatic ingredient of Crêpes Suzette. I used to love this pudding as a child but can't remember when I last had it.

When I was very young, my adored and eccentric godmother Rachel would occasionally sweep in from her home in Austria in a flurry of furs, shiny jewels, expensive scent and cigarette smoke and whisk me off for lunch at The Ritz. The routine was always the same. The waiter would hand us our menus and Rachel would wave them away, demanding to see the sweet trolley. She would peer at the Black Forest gateau, crème caramel, crème brûlée, pears in red wine and so on before dismissing them and asking whether it would be within the realm of the waiter's expertise to rustle up a decent Crêpes Suzette. Yes, he could stretch to such a thing. Only then would Rachel return to the menu and choose our starters and main courses. Knowing what dessert she had to look forward to was crucial, even if it was always the same one.

I loved the theatre of the Crêpes Suzette being flambéed at the table and I loved, too, the sip of Grand Marnier that my godmother insisted I had alongside it, despite my young age.

Grand Marnier was created in 1880 by Louis-Alexandre Marnier-Lapostolle and the recipe has remained the same over the centuries, a cognac base blended with exotic bitter orange essence. It's the most widely exported of all French liqueurs, shipped to 150 countries, and is particularly successful mixed in cocktails.

I like it best, though, either as a long drink with tonic, ice and a slice of orange (very refreshing in the summer) or sipped neat over ice after a fine dinner. One day I'll have it with Crêpes Suzette again.

40% vol; www.grand-marnier.com

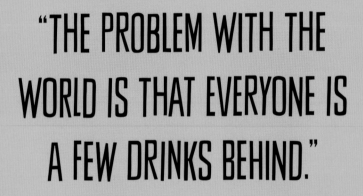

"THE PROBLEM WITH THE WORLD IS THAT EVERYONE IS A FEW DRINKS BEHIND."

HUMPHREY BOGART

GRANT'S MORELLA CHERRY BRANDY LIQUEUR ENGLAND

I was brought up in Kent in the southeast of England, and although I now live in Sussex, my heart remains in God's chosen county. I just have to see an oast house, hop garden or orchard – even just pictures in a twee National Trust calendar – and my heart quickens and my eyes prick with tears of nostalgia.

I'm a sucker, still, for the excellent produce of Kent: for Shepherd Neame's inimitable beers and ales; for Herbert Hall's and Chapel Down's astonishingly fine fizzes and for Kentish comestibles such Whitstable oysters; a Canterbury tart (oh stop it, behave, not that sort of tart; it's an apple tart as mentioned in Chaucer); and the magnificent Kent Korker sausage from Hoad's of Rolvenden.

To that list I must add this immaculate cherry brandy, first produced in Faversham, Kent, in 1774. I don't care what you say or what other cherry brandies you've had, there are none better than this.

As Alfred Jingle says in Dickens' *The Pickwick Papers*, 'Kent, sir – everybody knows Kent – apples, cherries, hops and women.' Well, this is the very cherry brandy that Jingle's friend Pickwick drinks in the book. It was Queen Victoria's favourite and it currently boasts a royal warrant from the Prince of Wales. We're talking top notch here.

Although nominally produced by Thomas Grant & Sons of Faversham, it is in fact now made by Shepherd Neame (the UK's oldest brewer, founded in 1698) from English grain spirit and Kentish cherries.

It's sweet, of course, and luscious, and fills the mouth with extraordinarily rich, fresh cherry flavours and a touch of almond and marzipan. It's perfect on its own, well-chilled after a meal, or splashed into a glass of Prosecco or Kentish fizz.

Or drink it as a so-called Percy Special. This savagely strong stirrup cup was invented by the 10th Duke of Northumberland for riders to hounds with the Percy Hunt. It's simply whisky and Grant's Cherry Brandy Liqueur, half and half, and, having just tried one – well, two, just to be sure – I can reveal that it rather creeps up on one and is not for the faint-hearted.

24% vol; www.shepherdneame.co.uk

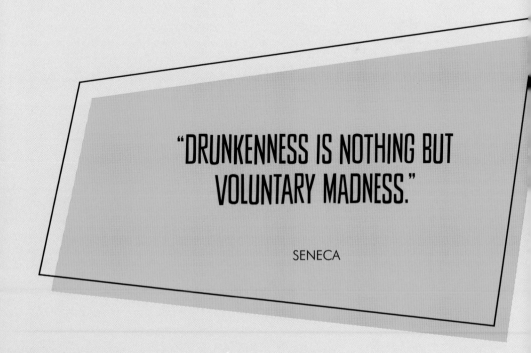

"DRUNKENNESS IS NOTHING BUT VOLUNTARY MADNESS."

SENECA

GREEN CHARTREUSE FRANCE

I remember that when I worked in Oddbins, Covent Garden, we had a wonderful old lady who lived upstairs, called Dolly. Back in the day she had been an actress of sorts and now in her dotage she spent her time reminiscing, collating old playbills and helping organize the entertainment sorority, the Grand Order of Lady Ratlings. Dolly was a good customer of ours and it was a rare day that we didn't see her. 'Only me!' she'd chirrup as she came bustling in for her sherry. Once a month she also bought a bottle of Green Chartreuse. 'It's what keeps me going, darling,' she'd explain cheerily. Convinced that it was the key to life, Dolly was in the habit of adding a large slug of it to her evening cocoa. Her purchases became more frequent so the slugs must have grown. There was clearly something to it, though, because she kept going well into her nineties.

Famously, Chartreuse has been produced in the Chartreuse Mountains near Grenoble, France, by Carthusian monks since 1737, using a recipe from a manuscript said to date from 1605 and possibly quite a bit earlier.

The original Chartreuse was known as the Élixir Végétal de la Grande-Chartreuse and is still made at an explosive 69% vol (you're meant to dilute it or eat a sugar cube soaked in it). Green Chartreuse, a naturally green liqueur made from 130 herbs and other plants macerated in alcohol, dates from 1764. The slightly sweeter, less alcoholic Yellow Chartreuse was added in 1838. The exact recipe is known to just two monks and they oversee everything from the picking of the plants to their maceration, distillation and ageing.

I like Green Chartreuse neat, ice cold or on the rocks after a meal. It works surprisingly well in several cocktails, too, the Bijou especially, which is one third each of Green Chartreuse, gin and sweet red vermouth with a splash of orange bitters, stirred over ice. I've also heard tell of the Black Wolf (Green Chartreuse, Black Sambuca and Tabasco), which sounds positively ghastly. I'd much rather try Dolly's mixture.

55% vol; www.chartreuse.fr

HAVANA CLUB AÑEJO ESPECIAL RUM
CUBA

The first thing I was offered on visiting the Havana Club Rum Museum in, erm, Havana, was a large, ice-cold glass of fresh sugar cane juice. It was incredibly sweet but wonderfully drinkable and refreshing. I couldn't stop licking my lips. 'Now you know why our rum is so good!' said a laughing Don José Navarro, the head distiller who was generously escorting me around. 'It's 100 per cent natural and 100 per cent full of goodness. But wait until you taste the rum. You won't stop smiling for days.'

I told Don José that I was a few days ahead of him in that respect and had already conducted my researches in El Floridita ('The Cradle of the Daiquiri') and La Bodeguita del Medio ('The Home of the Mojito'). And in the bar of the Hotel Sevilla – where Graham Greene set *Our Man in Havana* and where Capone stayed – and that of Hotel Ambos Mundos, too, where Hemingway began writing *For Whom the Bell Tolls*. Don José, I seem to remember, was suitably impressed by my diligence. And the point is that he was right: I'd not stopped grinning since I'd arrived in his fabulous city.

Havana Club is the world leader when it comes to rums in the super-premium and above category, exporting 50 million bottles a year to over 120 countries. The fabulous Havana Club Unión (the first ever rum made especially to match a Cuban cigar) had critics in a swoon on its release a couple of years back, as have the regular Havana Club Tributo Collection releases.

Rather more affordable is this little gem, the Añejo Especial. A molasses-based rum aged for up to five years in young oak barrels, it's soft, smooth, delicately sweet and full of rich vanilla flavours. It's the perfect mixer and is the rum that the Habanos use to make their ubiquitous Cuba Libres. Every home should have a bottle, if only for the smiles it will bring.

40% vol; https://havana-club.com

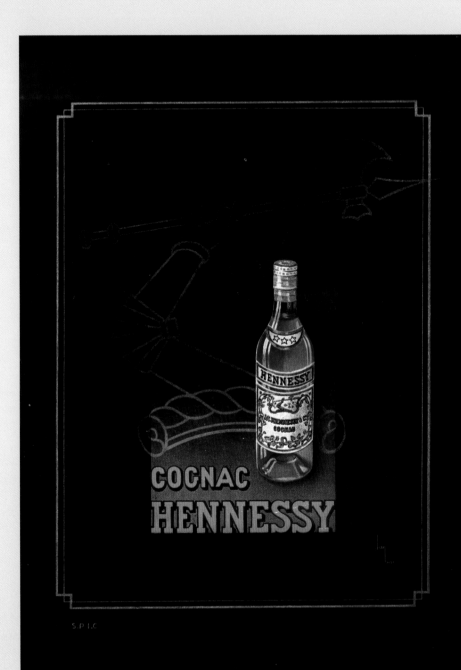

S.P.I.C

HENNESSY XO COGNAC FRANCE

Founded in 1765 by Richard Hennessy, an Irish officer in the army of Louis XV, Hennessy is the largest of all the cognac producers and exports almost every drop that it makes. The company might now be part of the vast Louis Vuitton Moët Hennessy empire but the founding family is still represented by global brand ambassador Maurice Hennessy of the eighth generation. And if one's in any doubt that they value consistency here, the master distiller, Yann Fillioux, is the seventh generation of his family in the role, his forebear having been employed by Richard Hennessy's son James in 1800.

It was Yann's grandfather who created this wonderful cognac, Hennessy XO (Extra Old), in 1870 especially for the personal consumption of Maurice's grandfather (also called Maurice) and Maurice's friends. A blend of some 100 different aged eaux-de-vie, it was the first ever cognac in this category and was deemed by Maurice to be so fine, so special and so – well – darn tasty that he would be a fool not to commercialize it. Hennessy XO has since become the benchmark against which other cognacs are judged.

Lovers of fine cognac have much to thank the Hennessys for. It was they who were asked to create a 'very superior old pale' cognac for the Prince Regent in 1817 and VSOP has now become a standard category. And in 1865 Maurice Hennessy started to give his cognacs a star rating and so the Three Star or VS (Very Special) category was born.

Anyway, back to the XO. This is still blended from around 100 different eaux-de-vie, each one of which must be at least six years old and in practice are anything up to 30 years old. It's a silky, sumptuously elegant cognac, but robust and powerful too. There's a sweetness to it, a warm vanilla nuttiness and an appealing earthiness. I sometimes get cocoa, dark coffee and sometimes a hint of toffee too. I always get pleasure.

40% vol; www.hennessy.com

HIBIKI SUNTORY WHISKY, JAPANESE HARMONY JAPAN

The first time I went to Japan I felt completely adrift.
I couldn't make head or tail of anything. There were no
links, no points of reference, no shared history, no common
culture. And, despite learning a few essential phrases on the
flight, I couldn't understand a word and nor could anyone
understand me. It started with me getting turfed off the train
from Narita Airport to Tokyo. The guard on the platform
looked at my ticket and ushered me onto the train. The
inspector on the train looked at my ticket and ushered me
onto the platform. On, off, on, off. This pantomime continued
for many minutes until I gave them both the slip and boarded
several carriages down and locked myself in the loo.

Tokyo itself was a shock: so crowded, so modern, so neon
and so, so thrilling. I checked in to my hotel and went straight
to the bar for a soothing Asahi lager. The UK and Japan are
both island nations, roughly the same size, I told myself. We
have a monarchy; they have a monarchy. We are formal and
polite; they are formal and polite. We drive on the left; they
drive on the left. We like gardening; they like gardening. We
drink tea; they drink tea. We make and drink whisky; they
make and drink whisky. Hang on a minute. Whisky!

The barman had studied in London and spoke beautiful
English. I explained how lost I felt. He looked at me and said
I could drink some Scotch and stay lost or I could drink some
Japanese whisky and start to learn. And so it was that I had
my first ever glass of Hibiki Harmony.

Make no mistake, this is thunderingly fine. A blend of grain
and malt whiskies from Suntory's Yamazaki, Hakushu and
Chita distilleries, it's Japan's most lauded blended whisky.
It's light, elegant and full of honey, herbs, chocolate,
preserved orange and much, much more. I envy anyone
sampling it for the first time.

43% vol; https://whisky.suntory.com

HIGHLAND PARK DRAGON LEGEND
SINGLE MALT SCOTCH WHISKY SCOTLAND

Hobbister Moor is the key to the whiskies of Highland Park. It's a blasted heath for sure and there are no trees on it to speak of. What trees there might once have been have simply been blown away. Indeed, it's said that whenever the roaring gales cease, people on Orkney topple over, so used are they to leaning into the ferocious winds.

Highland Park was established in 1798 and every expression in the range hits the spot for me, be it the 10 Year Old Viking Scars, the 12 Year Old Viking Honour, the 18 Year Old Viking Pride. The eagle-eyed amongst you might notice something of a theme developing here: Highland Park is nothing if not proud of its noble Norse heritage.

When it comes to making whisky, the distillery takes the view that all Scottish water is great, yeast is yeast and pretty much whatever top-quality barley is available will do. What's important and what makes Highland Park different from other whiskies is the peat with which it dries its barley.

Peat is the terroir of island whiskies and here on Hobbister Moor the peat is rich in decayed heather and rootlets. The lack of wood in its composition means that it burns slower at a lower temperature and with less smoke than most peats. By drying barley with smouldering peat you get a wonderful sweet, floral, smoky flavour and using this unique local peat is what Highland Park is all about.

With Dragon Legend they've turned up the peat to 11 and the whisky shows this off to perfection. It's intensely aromatic and smoky. It's richly spiced too with hints of fruitcake and vanilla. There's no getting away from it – it's a rough, tough and gruff, untamed whisky, wonderful in its wildness and it's perfectly suited to that Viking thing they've got going on.

43.1% vol; www.highlandparkwhisky.com

HINE HOMAGE XO COGNAC FRANCE

If you admire the cognacs of Thomas Hine & Co as I do, then you will love this. There's nothing like it anywhere else and it encapsulates exactly what the company is all about. It was created as a tribute to Thomas Hine himself, a Dorset man from Beaminster who had the misfortune to be banged up in Château Jarnac during the French Revolution on suspicion of being a spy. Happily, the French saw sense and released him; Hine saw sense too and married a local girl whose father – how lucky can you get? – owned a cognac company. Hine immersed himself in his father-in-law's business, became a skilled blender of cognacs and by the time he died in 1822, the company was known as Thomas Hine & Co.

As Hine fans will know, it's one of the smaller cognac producers and one of the few to source its cognacs exclusively from the two top crus of the Cognac region: Grande Champagne and Petite Champagne. The company only makes cognacs of VSOP quality and above and specializes in producing vintage cognacs – a rarity. Hine is also famous for producing so-called 'Early Landed' cognacs, a practice started at the beginning of the nineteenth century, whereby selected cognacs were shipped in cask to England. It was found that those cognacs matured in humid English cellars took on different characteristics to those matured in Jarnac: they were light, fruity and delicate rather than complex, woody and powerful. Hine continues to send certain casks to be aged in the deep, damp Wickwar cellars near Bristol, dug originally to provide stone cladding for tunnels along Brunel's Great Western Railway.

This glorious cognac is a marriage of English-matured and French-matured cognacs – specifically from the 1983, 1985, 1986 and 1987 vintages – and eaux-de-vie at least six years old, and the result is remarkably complex, enticing and rewarding. I should know, I'm sitting here sipping it now. There are hazelnuts, pears and honey on the nose and palate and definite notes of candied orange peel. It's a belter!

40% vol; www.hinecognac.com

ISLE OF HARRIS GIN SCOTLAND

I love absolutely everything about this gin. I love its strikingly beautiful bottle (twisted glass with a wooden cork stopper and a base of delicate blue); I love its artisanal paper label (flecked with copper); I love its unique flavour (infused with sugar kelp); I love its strength (45% vol); I love the fact that they like you to add a splash of sugar kelp aromatic water to it when drinking it neat (it adds a distinct note of the sea); I love its story (the Isle of Harris Distillery in Tarbert was built in 2015 to make whisky; gin-making fills the time whilst they wait for the whisky to mature).

Actually, hold on a sec, one thing I don't love is how complicated Isle of Harris Gin is to get hold of. For some reason, they like you only to buy it direct from the distillery or the distillery's own website rather than from the usual go-to places for lovers of fine spirits such as Master of Malt or the Whisky Exchange. I'm afraid it drops a mark here.

Oh, and I know my maths is hopeless so I've probably got this wrong but given that the gin retails for £37 ($50) per 70cl bottle and the sugar kelp aromatic water retails for £20 ($28) per 5cl bottle, this means that if the water was sold in the same size bottle as the gin, the water would retail for, erm, £280 ($380). Can that be right?!

These quibbles apart, it's a corkingly fine gin and a sensual delight to serve and to drink. And given that the sugar kelp aromatic water is created by that remarkable apothecary, Amanda Saurin, who can do no wrong in my eyes, they're forgiven. They use nine botanicals: juniper, coriander, cassia bark, angelica, bitter orange peel, cubeb, liquorice, orris root and the aforementioned and crucial sugar kelp, harvested from the deep by local diver Lewis Mackenzie.

Who'd have thought the Outer Hebrides would be home to such a magnificent gin? I can't wait for their inaugural Hearach whisky to be ready.

45% vol; www.harrisdistillery.com

JACK DANIEL'S SINGLE BARREL SELECT TENNESSEE WHISKEY USA

I almost died of thirst when I visited Jack Daniel's in Lynchburg, Tennessee. It was 100 degrees and as I sweated and sweltered my way round America's oldest registered distillery, I had an *Ice Cold in Alex* moment, fantasizing about how fine a chilled Mint Julep would be at the tour's end. Imagine my crushing disappointment, then, to find myself offered a glass of homemade lemonade. Sadly, in my excitement, I had forgotten that Jack Daniel's is produced in a so-called 'dry' county, a relic of Prohibition, and that you can't get a proper drink there for love nor money. For that you have to drive a dozen miles to Tullahoma. Crazy but true.

I doubt founder Jasper Newton Daniel (born c.1850) would have approved. Jack, as he was known, learned to distil as a boy whilst lodging with Dan Call, a moonshine-making Lutheran minister. By the time he was 16, Jack had bought Dan's pot still and, well, the rest is history.

Today, JD is made just as it always was, using corn, rye and malted barley, a little yeast and plenty of iron-free, limestone-filtered water. After distillation, the spirit is filtered drop by drop through ten feet of crushed sugar maple charcoal – taking a full six days to pass through – before being barrelled and matured in one of scores of warehouses dotted around Moore County. Thanks to savagely cold winters and scorching hot summers, the spirit is forced in and out of the wood of the barrel, gaining colour and character as it does so. It's said that two years' ageing in Tennessee is akin to 12 in Scotland.

Almost all the barrels are blended into Jack Daniel's Old No. 7 (the best-selling single whisky/whiskey brand in the world) but just occasionally they will happen upon a barrel of such exceptional quality that they bottle it unblended. This is just such a bottling, a strikingly fine whiskey full of toffee, butterscotch, spice and vanilla.

45% vol; www.jdsinglebarrel.com

JANNEAU GRAND ARMAGNAC VSOP
FRANCE

Janneau is one of the great names of armagnac and has been based in the ancient town of Condom in the heart of Gascony since the company's foundation in 1851. Yes, yes, I said Condom. Go on, let it all out, have a good giggle!

The house doesn't have any vineyards of its own but works instead with top-quality wine growers in Bas Armagnac and Ténarèze. There are ten grape varieties permitted in the region, the most important of which are Colombard, Folle Blanche, Ugni Blanc and Baco Blanc (aka Baco 22A) – a hybrid derived from Folle Blanche and the phylloxera-resistant American grape, Noah.

Janneau's master distiller, Philippe Sourbes, who has been with the company for over 35 years, picks the best possible wines from these grapes and ensures that each variety is distilled separately, using both the single continuous still so typical of the region (it's often known as the 'Armagnacais still') but also – and here's where Janneau differs from almost every other armagnac producer – the double pot still as used in Cognac. The spirit is then aged in 450-litre (100-gallon) oak casks in Janneau's cellars. Once Sourbes judges the brandies to be mature enough, they are blended together and aged again, this time for six months in vast wooden foudres.

I've always loved Janneau's armagnacs, especially the VSOP which is far and away their best seller. It's aged for a minimum four years and a maximum 20 and is bottled in the traditional and distinctive flask-shaped Basquaise bottle.

VSOP stands for Very Superior Old Pale, of course. It was in Condom – please *stop* that giggling – that I learned it also stands for *versez sans oublier personne* (pour without forgetting anybody). They're awfully polite, these Gascons.

40% vol; www.armagnac-janneau.com

JEAN-PAUL METTÉ EAU-DE-VIE DE POIRE WILLIAMS FRANCE

Alsace is my favourite region in all France. Well, equal favourite with Gascony. The land of castles and eaux-de-vie versus the land of d'Artagnan and armagnac. I guess it's a tie between the two.

As you know, Alsace lies in the far east of France, between the Vosges Mountains and the mighty River Rhine and it's had an extraordinary history. Thanks to dust-ups such as the Thirty Years' War, the French Revolution, the Franco-Prussian War and two world wars, it has switched between German and French control with dizzying regularity. Remarkably, though, its picture postcard-pretty medieval towns and villages such as Beblenheim, Colmar, Obernai, Ribeauvillé and Riquewihr remain intact, complete with twisting cobbled streets and colourful, half-timbered houses.

The climate is benign, the welcome warm, the food excellent and the wines, well, they're first rate and I could bang on about them indefinitely. There are crisp, dry Rieslings, headily spicy Gewurztraminers, lusciously aromatic Muscats and astonishingly fine sweet wines. Oh and the Pinot Noirs ain't bad either. What I always forget, though, until I'm in Alsace, is how much I enjoy their spirits too.

They distil all manner of fruit there, producing exceptional, richly scented, colourless spirits that make superb digestifs. If you've not had eau-de-vie de mirabelle or quetsch (both plum), coing (quince), framboise (raspberry), fraise (strawberry) or Poire William (pear) you're in for a real treat.

I discovered Jean-Paul Metté's Eau-de-Vie de Poire Williams only a few weeks ago when last in Colmar and it knocked my socks off. I'd never had anything as fine. The first time I smelt it, I was whisked straight back to my boyhood, sneaking into my neighbour's orchard to eat ripe pears straight from the tree. The sticky juice that would run down my chin and my arms smelt just like this.

Jean-Paul Metté (known locally as the Pope of Eaux-de-Vie) founded his small, artisanal distillery in Ribeauvillé in the 1960s and it's now owned and run by his godson, Philippe Traber and Philippe's family. Their entire range of eaux-de-vie is a complete delight. Nothing takes me back to Kent, circa 1972, quite like this though.

42% vol; www.distillerie-mette.com

"A WOMAN DROVE ME TO DRINK AND I NEVER EVEN HAD THE COURTESY TO THANK HER."

W.C. FIELDS

JINRO 24 SOJU SOUTH KOREA

This is — and I kid you not — the best-selling spirit brand in the world. Well, who'd have thought that? Apparently, they sell some 770 million bottles every year. Gosh.

Soju is a spirit that's usually distilled from fermented wheat, barley or rice although other starchy foods can be used and it can vary dramatically in strength from around 16% vol to 55% vol. It dates back to the thirteenth century when it was brought through Asia by invading Mongol hordes and today is a South Korean staple.

The largest producer of Soju is HiteJinro who have been making it since 1924. They market several different versions, or at least different strengths, and distil their Jinro from sweet potato, rice and, erm, tapioca. And, good grief, I've not had tapioca since I was a kid. Isn't that the stuff that looks like frogspawn that our mothers always forced us to eat just after sluicing some cod liver oil down us? Actually, don't laugh, for some reason there's a frog — or is it a toad? — depicted on the label. What on earth can that mean?

Jinro Soju is not unlike a not-very-strong vodka (it's just 24% vol, hence its name) and the producers recommend drinking it neat on the rocks (which is how most Koreans drink it), using it in cocktails or lobbing a shot of it into your beer (which they like to be known as a J-Beer).

You know what? It's not half bad. It's very much part of Korean culture, though, and I don't really see it catching on here. That being said, I used it to make a pretty decent cocktail last night using muddled fresh honeydew melon, some fresh ginger, fresh mint and a splash of Cointreau.

I'm not entirely sure that my drinks cupboard is crying out for this to be included in it, though. But if you have even half an interest in spirits you should try it.

24% vol; en.hitejinro.com

"ALCOHOL, TAKEN IN SUFFICIENT QUANTITIES, MAY PRODUCE ALL THE EFFECTS OF DRUNKENNESS."

OSCAR WILDE

JOHNNIE WALKER BLUE LABEL SCOTLAND

Johnnie Walker is the best-selling blended Scotch whisky by miles. And with reason: it's bloody good. It never disappoints no matter which of its many expressions you're drinking. The best-known are the Red Label, the Black Label, the Double Black, the Green Label, the Gold Label Reserve, the 18 Year Old and this, the Johnnie Walker Blue Label, launched in 1992, the star of the range and definitely my favourite.

I'm told that they sell 17 million cases of Johnnie Walker a year, which is a stupendous amount – that means one bottle of JW is sold somewhere in the world roughly every six seconds. Even by my reckoning, that's not bad going at all.

Johnnie Walker's owners, Diageo, have some 10 million casks of whisky maturing in their various distilleries and this gives them a remarkable palette to work with when it comes to creating their blends. Blue Label has no age statement but we know there are mature grain whiskies in it (possibly old stock from the now-closed Port Dundas and Cambus) plus malt from Benrinnes and Cardhu (both Speyside), Clynelish (Highlands) and Caol Ila (Islay).

Oh and, BTW, whilst we're on the subject, if you have trouble remembering the four whisky regions of Scotland, here's a handy mnemonic. Scotland has lots of hills, right? So, bearing that in mind, it's easy to remember that the regions are: Highland, Island, Lowland and Speyside. You can have that one on me. No, no, not at all, it's my pleasure.

Johnnie Walker Blue comes in a big, heavy bottle, leading one to assume the whisky will be big and heavy too. But, on the contrary, it's surprisingly light and delicate. There's a gentle whisper of smoke and hints of fresh apples and cut grass and the promise of baked shortbread and – I'm probably imagining it – Dundee Cake too. The bottle might be imposing and bold but the whisky within is far from being so – it's incredibly light on its feet and worth every penny.

40% vol; www.johnniewalker.com

Good work – good whisky

JOHNNIE WALKER

Born 1820 — still going strong

Printed by Sir Joseph Causton & Sons, Ltd., 68 Fleet Street, London, E.C. 4, and Eastleigh, Hants, and Published by The Field Press (1930) Ltd., 41, Southgate Street, Winchester, in the County of Southampton, Saturday, December 20, 1941. PRINTED IN GREAT BRITAIN and entered as second class matter at the Post Office, New York, N.Y., March 1897.

KETEL ONE CITROEN VODKA HOLLAND

And there was me thinking that Citroen was a car. Well it still is, I suppose, but it's also a rather fine flavoured vodka from Holland. I first came across it in the Oxo Tower Bar in London where it's one of the crucial ingredients of their signature Bloody Mary, along with tomato juice, lemon juice, PX sherry, slow roasted garlic cloves, smoked jalapeño chipotle peppers, Maldon sea salt and, erm, I think that's it.

The Ketel One Citroen provides the backbone to a drink that's about as complicated and as fine as you'll find and which – if you include the crudités and homemade horseradish dip it's served with – is almost a meal in itself.

Ketel One (named after the company's original – Number One – copper pot still, known in Dutch as a 'distilleerketel' or simply 'ketel') is made at the Nolet distillery in Schiedam in Holland, established in 1691 and owned and run, father to son, by ten generations of the Nolet family. Carolus Nolet is the current head with Carl Nolet and Bob Nolet in the wings representing the 11th generation.

Ketel One Citroen was launched in 2000 to considerable acclaim and there's no question that it's the best lemon vodka around. The vodka is produced from top-quality, 100 per cent GM-free winter wheat. It's fermented and distilled first in a column still and then part of the batch is redistilled in ten copper pot stills. The resulting spirit is crisp, clean and very, very smooth. This will then be blended and married and either bottled simply as Ketel One or turned into Ketel One Citroen by infusing it with the essence of four different types of lemon and two of lime.

It's a bracingly fresh vodka and although I do use it in Bloody Marys I like to keep a bottle in the freezer and enjoy ice-cold shots of it whenever the situation demands.

40% vol; www.ketelone.com

KI NO BI KYOTO DRY GIN JAPAN

Yes, yes, I know what you're thinking. You're thinking Star Wars and Obi-Wan Kenobi. Well you're way off target. It might sound the same but it's spelt differently. And it means something different too. Ki No Bi is Japanese for 'beauty of the seasons' and in this instance Ki No Bi is a thumpingly fine Japanese gin for which we must thank Messrs Marcin Miller and David Croll from Blighty. These two Brits (actually, Marcin is a London-born Pole) have some form in the world of spirits, having distributed Japanese whisky around the world very successfully through their Number One Drinks Co.

One day it dawned on them that Japan (where Croll now lives) would be the perfect place to make gin. Or, more specifically, Kyoto would be, it being the home of all manner of craft-made goods such as kimonos, sake, lacquer work and woodcuts. And so it was that they founded The Kyoto Distillery, the first to be built in Japan specifically to make gin.

Unsurprisingly, M and C couldn't find a Japanese gin distiller so they found themselves a Welsh one instead (as you do), Alex Davies – formerly of the Cotswolds and the Chase Distilleries and easy to spot in Kyoto, thanks to his ginger hair. They also took on Mas Onishi, the former distillery manager at Suntory's Yamazaki Distillery, as their technical advisor. Whilst waiting for the distillery to be built, the team created a library of some 60 distilled botanicals before honing their recipe to just 11, including yellow yuzu, hinoki (Japanese cypress) chips, green sansho berries, bamboo, cave-aged ginger, lemon from Hiroshima and hand-picked gyokuro tea from Uji. Only the juniper and orris root are imported.

The botanicals are distilled in six flavour categories to maximize aromatic intensity and a rice-based spirit is used, giving a noticeable sake-like softness and sweetness to the gin. And it's this unexpected idiosyncrasy that marks Ki No Bi out. It's gin all right, but unlike anything else I've had before. And I love it: gin with a twist, from a country far, far away.

45.7% vol; www.kyotodistillery.jp

ESSENTIAL HOME COCKTAIL KIT

Take a gander behind the back bar of your favourite watering hole and you will be astounded at the amount of kit they have. I've seen fewer tools and less hardware in my local hospital emergency department.

But don't panic. A lot of what the professionals like to have close to hand is superfluous for amateur bartenders such as you and me. Besides, you will be surprised to find that you have most of what you need in the kitchen already.

A cocktail shaker of some sort is essential. I stick to the Boston shaker, which is the most useful. You can pick one up (the glass and tin version anyway) pretty cheaply. Heavier glass and steel ones are much more, whilst retro-chic ones can cost the earth. But you can't hope to make any decent shaken cocktails without one, although in extremis you can use two differently sized beer glasses. Oh, and you'll need a proper Hawthorne strainer to go with it – the one with the coiled wire round the edge. You can buy these online for peanuts.

You will also need a very sharp knife for cutting fruit; a wooden chopping board; a lemon squeezer; a lemon zester (a potato peeler will do); a muddler/pestle; a jug (pitcher); some non-plastic straws; a crown cap bottle opener; some cocktail sticks; a jar of olives; a jar of cocktail onions; celery salt; Lea & Perrins Worcestershire sauce; Angostura Bitters; Tabasco; a measuring jigger (25ml/1fl oz one end and 50ml/1¾fl oz the other) and a long-handled julep spoon.

Hang on, don't fret! I bet you have all of these, bar the last two, tucked away in your kitchen or larder. And don't you go worrying about not having an ice bucket either. I don't have an ice bucket. I do have two freezer drawers full of ice, though, which I call upon as and when.

As for alcohol, no amateur cocktail bar should be without, at the very least, one bottle each of vodka, gin, whisky, bourbon, cognac, triple sec; Campari; and dry white, sweet white and sweet red vermouth.

You will also need fresh lemons, limes and oranges, mixers, a bottle of Grenadine or sugar syrup/sirop de gomme and I strongly suggest that you invest in some 1kg sachets of Funkin's excellent fruit purées. All bartenders use them; they come in a vast range of flavours (such as white peach, strawberry, raspberry, lemon and so on) and contain only freshly pulped fruit and sugar. They last for up to eight days after opening and are perfect for all manner of fruit-based cocktails.

You will need a number of martini glasses, of course, some highball glasses, Old Fashioned glasses or tumblers and champagne flutes and that should be about it.

Most importantly, though, don't forget the other two essentials for successful cocktail making: imagination and a raging thirst.

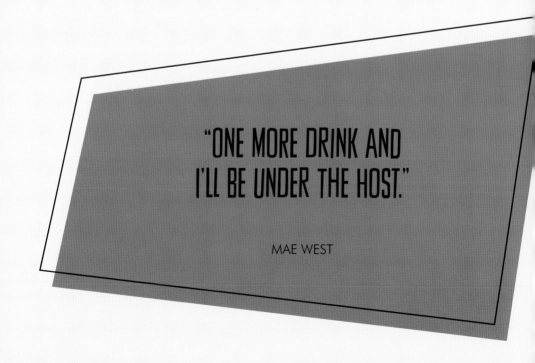

"ONE MORE DRINK AND I'LL BE UNDER THE HOST."

MAE WEST

KILCHOMAN NEW SPIRIT BRAMBLE LIQUEUR SCOTLAND

Kilchoman (kill-homn) Distillery is one of the new kids on the block. Built on the all but derelict Rockside Farm on Islay – just a mile or so from Bruichladdich (page 36) – it launched in 2005, the first new distillery on the island for 125 years.

You might well have come across the Kilchoman Machir Bay single malt with its peaty smoke, rich fruity core and its hearty character thanks to time spent in former bourbon and oloroso sherry casks. Very unusually, they grow their own barley here rather than buy it in and they use their own traditional floor maltings. The whisky is then distilled, matured and bottled here; they have full control of every single part of the whisky-making process and not many distilleries can boast that.

And not many distilleries can boast such a tasty whisky liqueur as this. Indeed, apart from Drambuie (page 58), I find very few whisky liqueurs that appealing. They're either too sweet or too unbalanced and simply taste artificially confected. This, though, is spot on and is delightfully un-mucked about with, being made simply by macerating fresh blackberries (brambles) in Kilchoman new spirit, malt whisky and honey.

It's delightfully complex with the richness, fruitiness and downright juiciness of the blackberries underpinned – spoiler alert! – by massive, nay enormous, smoky peat notes and suggestions of honey. Somehow, it just works.

I like it best neat on the rocks, before or after a meal, or as a long drink with plenty of tonic and ice. The mixology mastermind known as Mr Lyan (aka Ryan Chetiyawardana) suggests serving it as Smoked Summer Spritz. Simply mix 25ml (1fl oz) Bramble Liqueur with 30ml (1fl oz) Campari and serve over ice in a highball glass topped up with soda. It's a smoke bomb all right and if smoke is your thing you'll love it. In any event, it sure beats a cigarette.

19% vol; www.kilchomandistillery.com

THE KING'S GINGER LIQUEUR HOLLAND

Produced exclusively for stately St. James's Street wine merchant Berry Bros & Rudd (Est: 1698) by De Kuyper Royal Distillers (Est: 1695) in Holland, The King's Ginger Liqueur recipe was concocted in 1903 by the then Mr Berry and the then doctor to King Edward VII. The king had recently taken delivery of his new horseless carriage – a Daimler no less – and it was felt that a nip of ginger would be just the thing to keep the poor chap protected from the elements as he pootled about in his motor.

Made from top-quality ginger root and lemon oils, it comes in at a bold 41% vol and is alarmingly moreish, being sweet and gingery in the mouth, oily and unctuous. The sweetness then fades to a wonderfully dry, fiery, spicy finish. It's spectacular on its own – either neat from a hipflask or in a tumbler on the rocks – and makes an excellent addition to all manner of cocktails. It's also ridiculously tasty poured over vanilla ice cream.

When I worked at Berrys', I remember that we once had sixties popstar Adam Faith to lunch. We were trying out a new cook and she was anxious to impress and insisted on producing her signature first course: quails' eggs in champagne aspic. This was followed by steak and chips, cheese and the aforementioned ice cream drenched in KGL. Mr Faith gave the starter a wide berth, I noticed, and didn't touch the steak. He picked at a few chips, had a morsel of cheese and wolfed down the pudding. He then made his excuses and left.

I later called his PA to check that all was well since our guest had seemed a little underwhelmed by proceedings. Not to worry, I was told, Adam had had a lovely time. He particularly liked 'the sweet with the gingery sauce' and wanted to order a dozen bottles of the liqueur. He was rather surprised, though, by the starter and reckoned that a company such as Berrys' had no business serving sheeps' eyes in jelly to guests.

41% vol; www.thekingsginger.com

101

CHÂTEAU DE LAUBADE XO BAS ARMAGNAC FRANCE

Gascony in southwest France is a glorious spot and one that I visit as often as I can. It's where the incomparable d'Artagnan came from, of course, and so strangely untouched is Gascony — with its crumbling châteaux, its tiny medieval hamlets and villages, its sweeping meadows, its fields of vibrant yellow sunflowers, its forests of ancient oaks and its rolling vineyards — that if I saw the fourth musketeer come trotting down the road on his famously ridiculous-looking horse, I wouldn't be in the least surprised.

Château de Laubade (very much a château of the non-crumbling sort) was built in 1870 in the heart of Bas Armagnac and it's the leading armagnac estate, boasting famous old vintages in its cellars dating back to 1855. It has been owned for the last three generations by the Lesgourgues family and they take quality seriously here. Only grapes grown on the family's 105-hectare (260-acre) single vineyard (the largest in the region) are used in production. The estate is farmed organically and it's the only armagnac producer to have its own cooperage, using only the finest Gascon oak.

The eaux-de-vie in Château de Laubade XO are between 15 and 20 years old and they make for a richly-flavoured and complex glass of armagnac with toast, honey, nuts, tobacco, cinnamon and citrus peel on both nose and palate, backed by a long earthy, robust finish.

I know it's not cheap but I reckon it's still a bargain for what it is, especially so if you consider what the equivalent, sleek, shiny XO thoroughbreds from down the road in Cognac would cost.

40% vol; www.chateaudelaubade.com

LILLET BLANC FRANCE

I first came across Lillet Blanc years ago on a trip to Bordeaux and it remains one of my all-time favourite aperitifs. Mrs Ray adores it too and woe betide me if I forget to bring her some back whenever I'm in that neck of the woods. It seems not to have occurred to her that she could simply pick up a bottle from the supermarket when she does her weekly gin shop. Still, I don't want to encourage her to be any more of a lush than she already is.

Lillet Blanc is a so-called aromatized wine that has been produced in Podensac, a small village in the Graves region of Bordeaux, since 1872. Blended from wines made from Sémillon and Sauvignon Blanc and some zesty citrus liqueurs distilled from sweet and bitter oranges, it has an added touch of quinine and spends several months in oak before being bottled. Delicately sweet with honeyed notes, hints of pine resin and candied orange, Lillet Blanc is deeply refreshing served on ice with a slice of orange or as a long drink with ice and tonic. The richer, slightly sweeter Lillet Rouge and the lively, beautifully coloured Lillet Rosé (launched in 2012) are also both extremely tasty and satisfying.

Lillet Blanc is most famous, of course, as part of the classic Vesper Martini which James Bond orders in *Casino Royale* and which he later names after Vesper Lynd, the sexpot double agent to whom he takes something of a shine. In the book, the recipe is described as three measures of Gordon's Gin, one of vodka (brand unspecified) and half a measure of Kina Lillet (as it was then called), shaken over ice and served with a thin slice of lemon, and jolly good it is too.

Lillet is also integral to the finest of the several different versions of that infallible hair-of-the-dog cocktail, the Corpse Reviver. This contains Lillet, gin, triple sec, absinthe, lemon juice and sugar syrup and, as Mrs Ray and I have discovered many a time, it's enough to get even the most recalcitrant of hungover corpses twitching back to life.

17% vol; www.lillet.com

LUXARDO SAMBUCA DEI CESARI ITALY

Sambuca was a staple of the seventies and I got a taste of it in my mid-teens, thanks – inevitably – to my father, who at the time was helping devise the wine lists of the Café Royal Grill Room in Regent Street, W1, and Jules Bar in Jermyn Street, SW1. In return, he was given a number of free meals a year.

My old man was often strapped for cash, so this led to the curious situation whereby – whenever my mother was away – our meals were a choice of tournedos Rossini at the Grill Room, filet mignon at Jules Bar or sardines on toast at home.

The trouble was that, when in a restaurant, my elderly father had the infuriating habit of inviting any passing girl, be it fellow diner or waitress, to come and join our table and 'chat to the boy' or – most embarrassing of all – noticing if a picture was hanging in any other manner than dead straight and demanding that it be corrected. 'Dear chap,' he would say to me, 'Do you see that picture over there on the far wall? The one behind that table of four. Be a good fellow and straighten it would you? It's a fraction down on the left.' I wasn't allowed back to the table until he was satisfied it was straight, bellowing across the room his instructions, much to my agony and everyone else's great amusement.

One of the beauties of the Grill Room was that there were no pictures to straighten, just mirrors set in the walls, red plush drapes and gold leaf Rococo caryatids. One of the other beauties was that the lovely maitre d', Carlo Ambrosini, always stood us a digestif on the house, invariably a glass of Luxardo Sambuca. I loved it when the glasses appeared wordlessly by our elbows. I loved it when Carlo lit three coffee beans in the glass as tradition dictated and I loved its syrupy sweet aniseed flavours and grew to like its bitter finish.

Best of all, drinking Sambuca in those days with my father made me feel like the grown up I was then far from being.

38% vol; www.luxardo.it

MAGNÍFICA DE FARIA CACHAÇA BRAZIL

I'm mad about cachaça. It lifts one up in a way that no other spirit can – it's little wonder the Brazilians are such a delightfully chipper lot.

Of all the many cachaças I've tried, this is my runaway favourite. I first came across it in Las Iguanas, the chain of 50 or so Latin American restaurants dotted around the UK. I was so bowled over by it that I felt compelled to tell the company's then owner, Ajith Jaya-Wickrema. He was so bowled over by the fact that I was so bowled over that he felt compelled to invite me to Brazil to see where it was made. It won't surprise you to learn that I felt compelled to accept.

A week or so later I was in a sugar cane plantation northeast of Rio de Janeiro where I discovered that simplicity is the key. Sugar cane is cut by hand and the stalks run through a mangle-like press. The juice is fermented in a steel tank and the resulting 'wine' (of around 11% vol) is then distilled in a copper alembic still. And that's it. The cane used at Magnífica is organically grown and the only thing they add is pure spring water. It's about as natural a spirit as there is.

I'm not sure I needed to fly to Rio to learn all this, but then if I hadn't, I wouldn't have had the joy of later finding myself on Copacabana Beach researching the many delights of the Caipirinha, that exquisite cocktail in which cachaça is the key ingredient. Again, simplicity is the key, the classic Caipirinha being made by cutting up a fresh lime into eight equal wedges, adding two teaspoons of caster sugar and then 'muddling' it with a pestle in a glass. Add 50ml (1¾fl oz) cachaça, top with crushed ice, bung in a straw and serve. What on earth could be easier or tastier?

You can ring the changes by using a fresh orange and grated ginger, or passion fruit, or mint and pineapple, or, crikey, whatever. To ensure the Caipirinha's complete success, though, you definitely need Magnífica Cachaça.

38% vol; www.cachacamagnifica.rio

MAKER'S 46 KENTUCKY BOURBON WHISKY USA

It's amazing that Maker's Mark ever saw the light of day. The founder, Bill Samuels Sr, had turned his back on bourbon and sold the family distilling firm of TW Samuels in 1943. Luckily for us, though, Bill was a lousy businessman. When he opened a bank with the proceeds it closed within two months and when he subsequently tried to make it as a car dealer, he failed again.

It was then that Bill's wife Marjorie told him to get a grip and return to distilling. She so inspired him that Bill vowed to do just that. And to prove that he would do so from scratch he promptly set fire to the family's treasured 170 year-old bourbon recipe, taking the parlour curtains with it, and – so family lore goes – almost one daughter too.

Bill bought Burk's Distillery in Loretto, Kentucky, in 1953 and started by baking bread. He discovered that red winter wheat made a more palatable, less bitter, loaf than rye and so, unlike his competitors, he used it instead of rye in his whisky (which, in a nod to his Scottish forebears, he spelt without the 'e').

And rather than the harsh steam-hammer that everyone else used to crush their grain, Bill used the gentler roller mill. He also determined to make his whisky in batches of no more than 19 barrels. Marjorie designed the bottle, the labels and the now-famous red wax top.

Today the company is owned by Beam Suntory with Bill's grandson, Rob Samuels, the COO. Everything is still done by hand, from milling to distillation, from rotating the barrels in the warehouse (to ensure even maturation) to the tearing of the labels and the dipping of said wax top.

Maker's Mark is a famously approachable bourbon – soft, mellow and fruity – and I love it. Thanks to the canny use of heavily charred French oak staves within each bespoke barrel, this Maker's 46 (the figure refers to the number of different levels of char they tried before happening on the ideal one) is a bigger, bolder, richer and more complex expression. It's also ridiculously enjoyable.

47% vol; www.makersmark.com

"THERE IS NO BAD WHISKEY. THERE ARE ONLY SOME WHISKEYS THAT AREN'T AS GOOD AS OTHERS."

RAYMOND CHANDLER

MENTZENDORFF KUMMEL FRANCE

Kummel, the luscious, caraway seed-based digestif first distilled in Holland in the late sixteenth century by one Lucas Bols, has long been one of my preferred after-dinner or, if the whole day is to be written off, after-lunch tipples.

I simply love it and although the likes of Wolfschmidt, Bols and De Kuyper Royal Distillers make excellent examples, my all-time favourite remains Mentzendorff, produced in the tiny Combier distillery in Saumur in the Loire Valley to the original 1823 recipe, created when the company (currently owned by Champagne Bollinger) was first established near Riga, Latvia.

The ten-strong team at Combier make many fine spirits such as the original triple sec, a fabulous cherry liqueur and several excellent, this'll-put-hair-on-your-chest absinthes. They're rather baffled by the kummel, though, since nobody in France appears to drink it.

For those yet to discover its delights, kummel is perhaps best described as grown-ups' gripe water, that ancient remedy for colic and general indigestion in children. The plant that gives both gripe water and kummel their distinctive aniseed-like flavour is caraway, a well-known carminative noted for easing gastrointestinal discomfort. And that's the thing: kummel really does help one digest in a way other spirits don't. Little wonder it's so popular with elderly, dyspeptic gents in golf clubs across the land, where it's known as 'putting mixture'.

Best served straight from the freezer or on the rocks, Mentzendorff Kummel is syrupy sweet at first, after which the spicy aniseed note kicks in, followed by a deliciously pure, dry finish that soothes and comforts all the way down. It's sublime. It's excellent in cocktails like the Silver Streak (two parts gin; one part kummel), the Quelle Vie (two parts cognac; one part kummel) and the mock Negroni (one part kummel; one part gin; one part red vermouth; two dashes of Angostura bitters). Oh and you can now also get it in 150cl magnums...

38% vol; www.mentzendorff.co.uk

MIXERS

I owe Fever Tree Tonic Water a massive vote of thanks and I'd wager that you do too. For years I thought that I hated gin. When experimenting with alcohol as a precocious teen I drank it (invariably Gordon's) neat or with Rose's Lime Cordial simply to show off and simply to get pissed. When I graduated to posh drinks parties and drank gin with tonic, ice and a slice like one was supposed to, I despaired because I never really liked the taste (although I did love the smell of neat Beefeater) and thought I'd never fit in with my G&T-loving peers. It turns out, of course, that it was the crappy tonic I hated, not the gin.

Thanks to the launch of its first tonic water in 2005, Fever Tree revolutionized our drinking habits. There's no doubt in my mind at all that without Fever Tree there would have been no renewed passion for gin. Without FT there would have been no revolution. Fellow ginistas rise up and give praise!

As Fever Tree pointed out a dozen years ago, if you're going to spend a small fortune on a bottle of fine, bespoke spirits, why drown it in terrible tonic or dodgy ginger ale? Fever Tree alone makes seven different tonic waters these days, not to mention many other fine mixers. But, of course, where they led, others followed and there are now scores of excellent examples on the market.

Fentimans, Folkington, Franklin, Luscombe, London Essence, Merchant's Heart, to name a few, all make wonderful tonic waters, bitter lemons, ginger ales, ginger beers, colas, lemonades and so on. As much devotion goes into them as goes into the finest of handmade, craft distillery spirits.

To take one other example, the incomparable Amanda Saurin's Fierce Botanics Apothecary Tonic No.1 tonic is made from fresh, hand-gathered rose petals, citrus peel, juniper, Cinchona bark, spruce, fir and organic cane sugar. It might sound poncey but – crikey – it's good! I'm told it's even pretty tasty on its own as an alcohol-free libation although I'd never dream of not adding some gin, vodka or rum.

Many of the spirits within these pages are best enjoyed neat. Many, though, are best enjoyed with a mixer in which case I beg you not to cut corners. If you're prepared to splash out on the hooch, splash out on the mixer too. There's really no reason not to.

METHOD AND MADNESS SINGLE POT STILL IRISH WHISKEY IRELAND

I think I'm what Irish folk refer to pejoratively as a 'Plastic Paddy', that's to say someone with no connection to the Emerald Isle at all (other than, in my case, a cousin who lives in the north) who wishes he'd been born there. Well, I don't care; I love the place and – before family life intervened – used to travel there a lot.

Dublin was always the first port of call, of course, specifically Doheny & Nesbitt in Lower Baggot Street. A subsequent quickie in James Toner's would be followed by a half in O'Donoghue's and a swift one in Reilly's Bar opposite. A head-clearing stroll down Grafton Street would then lead to a gentle refresher in McDaid's. The welcomes would be warm, the Guinness ice-cold and the whiskey just so. I would be in absolute heaven.

Then it would be off to the further reaches of the island. To Wexford, say, for oysters and opera, to Galway for a flit to the Aran Islands, to Donegal for, well, for goodness knows what (and when I know you better I'll tell you about that time in Nancy's Bar in Ardara) and to Cork, of course, for whiskey.

Irish Distillers (owned by Pernod Ricard) has a space-age distillery about 25 kilometres (15 miles) east of Cork City in Midleton and it's where they produce such whiskeys as Jameson, Redbreast, Green Spot, Midleton, Powers, Dunphy's and so on.

It's also where they make this little eye-catcher, one of four brand new releases in their deeply experimental Method and Madness range created as much by the apprentice distillers as by the master distillers.

A single pot still whiskey matured in both oloroso sherry and bourbon casks, it's finished in chestnut casks from France, which is a first as far as I know.

As they at Midleton themselves say, it's a combination of what they've always done and what they've never done before, and I'd say they've pulled it off brilliantly. The whiskey is fabulously full-flavoured with sweetness from the chestnut, and toffee, preserved fruit and spice from the sherry and bourbon casks. It gives me yet another reason to love Ireland.

46% vol; www.methodandmadnesswhiskey.com

"ALWAYS DO SOBER WHAT
YOU SAID YOU'D DO DRUNK.
THAT WILL TEACH YOU TO KEEP
YOUR MOUTH SHUT."

ERNEST HEMINGWAY

MR BLACK COLD BREW COFFEE LIQUEUR
AUSTRALIA

I don't drink much coffee any more. Or tea, come to that. It's just that I've belatedly realized that I don't like non-alcoholic hot drinks. That's not to say that I like alcoholic hot drinks, though. I don't. Mulled wine, for example, is a travesty. Heating up cheap red wine simply gives you heated-up cheap red wine and why waste the expensive stuff? No, what I mean is that I only really like cold alcoholic drinks.

But when I say I don't drink coffee, I do drink this. And as for my wife, Marina, I have to ration it for her, poor lamb, and keep it under lock and key because she's developing something of a habit.

Mrs Ray and I would occasionally have a nip of Patrón XO Café Tequila after supper and darn good it is too. This though is even better. I mean, it's stunning.

A blend of just four ingredients – Australian grain spirit, Arabica coffee beans, water and sugar – it was launched in 2013 by distiller Philip Moore and designer Tom Baker who both shared a desire, as they put it, to take Australian coffee culture into the night.

They say it has half the sugar and ten times the coffee concentration of other coffee liqueurs and at 25% vol it's not ridiculously alcoholic (Patrón XO is 35% vol). There's enough to give you a pleasant buzz though and enough caffeine too (apparently a 30ml/1fl oz pour contains about 40 per cent of the caffeine found in a single espresso).

You can drink it neat over ice, you can splash milk or cream in if you really have to, or you can make a tip-top espresso martini with it. Once opened, the bottle lasts for ages (though not in this house) and as Messrs Moore and Baker point out, it's conveniently shaped to slip neatly into your fridge door.

25% vol; www.mrblack.co

MOUNT GAY XO RUM
BARBADOS

You have to be on your guard when drinking rum in Barbados. Visitors might drink it in cocktails or punches but the locals like to knock it back neat. If you want to blend in, you do as they do and buy it by the bottle (not necessarily 75cl; smaller sizes are permissible) alongside which you get a bowl of ice and a couple of glasses. You then drink it as it is followed by a shot of water, Coke, Sprite or even beer.

I spent an evening 'liming' with some locals; that's to say chatting late into the night and drinking far, far too much rum and far, far too little water, Coke, Sprite or even beer. My host had been in situ longer than I had and was even wobblier on his pins by the time we left. He offered to drive me back to my hotel but, thankfully, I was just sober enough to realize this was a bad idea. Notoriously, in this land of heavy rum drinkers, there are no laws at all against drink driving.

The finest rum on Barbados is, of course, Mount Gay, the longest-established rum distillery in the world. The oldest surviving deed from the company shows that it was in operation as early as 1703 and it was probably established years before that. They use molasses and two methods of fermentation (uncontrolled in open air vats and controlled in sealed ones) and two systems of distillation (double distillation in copper pot stills for body and robustness and continuous single distillation in column stills for smoothness and elegance). The two distillates are then aged separately in oak barrels, blended together, aged again and bottled.

Eclipse is the celebrated entry-level rum, beloved of mixologists and rum-lovers everywhere and at the other end of the Mount Gay scale is this magnificent XO. A blend of 7- to 15-year-old rums, it's richly flavoured, soft, smooth, toffee-rich and beautifully balanced and, for what it is, ridiculously well priced. Just leave the car behind.

43% vol; www.mountgayrum.com

NARDINI GRAPPA MANDORLA ITALY

It was in Bassano del Grappa, a striking medieval town in Vicenza, in the far northeast of Italy, that I saw the light.

The town is best known for its covered wooden bridge, built by Andrea Palladio in 1569. The Ponte Vecchio or Ponte degli Alpini has been damaged several times over the years, most notably during the Napoleonic Wars (during which the town was occupied twice by the French and twice by the Austrians) and in World War Two, when it was all but destroyed by retreating Germans. It was rebuilt in 1947 to Palladio's plans and is quite a sight.

I was drawn to the bridge not by its dramatic history (you can still see the bullet holes of Napoleon's soldiers in its walls), but by the allure of the Grapperia Nardini, sited at its eastern end ever since family-owned Bartolo Nardini, the oldest grappa producer in Italy, was founded in 1779. This café/bottle shop opens at 8A.M. every day to serve locals quick sharpeners on their way to work and it was there that I was introduced to the delights of the caffè corretto and the rasentin. My life has never been the same since.

The former is a shot of espresso coffee 'corrected' by the addition of some grappa and slips down an absolute treat. The latter is even more tasty, a shot of espresso and sugar that you down before the sugar has dissolved, after which you quickly rinse out the cup with a hearty slug of grappa. It's astonishingly delicious, the warmth of the cup, the headiness of the spirit, the bitterness of the coffee and the crunchiness of the sugar all combining to give a perfect taste sensation.

The ideal grappa to use is this exquisite almond-flavoured one, my absolute favourite in the excellent Nardini range. Intense and dry with a delicately sweet almond finish, it's perfect with both serves. And, as I discovered, it's even better on its own. I should have left it there that day and not had a second just to check. By 9.15A.M. I was completely smashed.

50% vol; www.nardini.it

NIKKA COFFEY MALT WHISKY JAPAN

Our whisky-loving parents and grandparents would be astonished. Where they just drank Scotch, possibly Irish or – at a pinch, in a cocktail – bourbon, we topers today have deliciously drinkable examples from all over the world to tempt us, many of which you will meet in these pages. I mean, who in Britain 30 years ago would have considered drinking whisky from India, Washington State, Switzerland, Texas or Japan? *Japan?* Are you crazy?

Well, if you're still in any doubt at all about the quality of Japanese whisky, just you have sip of this. It'll knock your socks off. My chum Dawn Davies MW, head buyer for The Whisky Exchange, who knows pretty much all there is to know about the subject, has just one word to describe it: awesome. I can't help but agree. And there's a nice story behind it too.

Masataka Taketsuru, born in 1894 to a family of sake-makers in Hiroshima, travelled to Britain and fell in love with Scotland, a Scottish girl and Scottish whisky. He enrolled at the University of Glasgow and studied chemistry. As an apprentice at a succession of distilleries, he studied, too, how to make whisky – the first Japanese person to do so. Masataka married the Scottish girl – Jessie Cowan, known as Rita – in 1920 and took his new bride and new-found knowledge back to Japan where he helped set up Suntory's Yamazaki Distillery and, in doing so, helped found the Japanese whisky industry. Ten years later Masataka set up his own distillery and in 1940 he launched his first Nikka whisky.

This Nikka Coffey Malt Whisky is a stunning tribute to Masataka. Distilled from malted barley at Nikka's Miyagikyo Distillery in the northeast of Honshu, using not the expected pot stills but two continuous Coffey stills (normally used for grain whisky) imported from Scotland, it's a remarkable dram. Rich, fruity and full, there are distinct notes of honey, bananas, cream and vanilla backed by a long, lingering finish. It's easy-going, yes, but it makes you think too. It certainly makes you think of Masataka and his Scottish bride.

45% vol; www.nikka.com

NORDIC AKEVITT BLANK NORWAY

The Oslo Håndverksdestilleri (OHD) was founded in 2015 by Marcin Miller (yep, the same guy behind the Ki No Bi Japanese gin on page 97) and Marius Vestnes of Cask Norway, an importer/exporter of fine beers and spirits. They were later joined by Martin Krajewski (owner of such tip-top wineries as Clos Cantenac in St Émilion, Château Séraphine in Pomerol and Aristea in South Africa).

Miller knows a thing or two about hard liquor. He is, after all, co-founder of *Whisky Magazine*, a Kentucky Colonel (thanks to his efforts in spreading the word about bourbon) and a Master of the Quaich (ditto with Scotch). He is also extremely skilled in spotting gaps in the spirits market that others either might not notice or might not have the energy to pursue.

And so when Miller found himself in northern Norway, among the lakes and the reindeer, chipping away at a block of pure glacial ice the better to chill his evening G&T whilst staying in Vestnes's cabin, he had a light-bulb moment: how best to distil and capture this very essence of Norway?

A couple of years later and the trio had built and opened in Oslo the first private distillery in Norway since the government established its drinks monopoly in the 1920s. It has been a resounding success. They started by distilling gin before turning their eyes to the ancient Nordic drink, akvavit. They make an excellent aged version matured for 12 months in American oak casks and they make this lighter version, the Akevitt Blank, made to be drunk neat or used in cocktails.

A selection of nine herbs and spices are used, all foraged locally, namely caraway, meadowsweet, heather flower, angelica, juniper, sorrel, calamus root, camomile and St John's wort. These combine superbly to create a fresh, slightly creamy, gently spicy, aniseed-redolent mouthful. It makes a deliciously quirky aperitif when drunk neat on the rocks or mixed with tonic as a long drink and is brilliant in cocktails where otherwise you might use gin or vodka. Do try it!

45% vol; www.oslodistillery.com

OCHO REPOSADO SINGLE ESTATE TEQUILA MEXICO

Oh come on, we've all done it. Found ourselves in some dive at 4A.M. – the last stragglers of a once merry band of brothers – slumped at a bar, trying to outdo each other with shots of tequila, downed in one after a suck of lemon, a lick of salt and a count of three. Happily, times have changed. Not only have we grown up (well, a bit) but our approach to tequila has also developed. It's still a fine ingredient in cocktails of course (I do love a good Margarita), but these days it's more likely to be drunk neat, not knocked back in a rush but lingered over and savoured. There's a style of tequila to suit everyone and it's quite possible to see four people at a bar drinking four completely different versions. It's rare to get such flexibility with a spirit (other than with rum, perhaps).

This is the first tequila to declare a vintage and is one of the exciting new terroir-driven tequilas made artisanally by legendary 'tequilero' Carlos Camarena in cahoots with Tomas Estes (known as 'Mr Tequila') at La Alteña Distillery in Jalisco. And remarkable it is too. Made from 100 per cent eight-year-old blue agave from one specific year (2017) and one specific field (which won't be harvested again for eight years), it's a Reposado, i.e. a 'rested' tequila which, in this case, has spent eight weeks and eight days (it's called Ocho – Eight – how many hints do you need?) in American oak barrels.

Bartenders love it because it's so light, fresh, wondrously smooth and deliciously adaptable. I like to drink it alongside my homemade sangrita which, strictly speaking, should accompany tequila Blanco rather than Reposado but I think we can get away with it. Authentic Mexican sangrita omits tomato juice but, well, this is my take on it: simply mix 15ml (1 tbsp) fresh lime juice, 20ml (4 tsp) fresh orange juice, 15ml (1 tbsp) grenadine, 50ml (1¾fl oz) tomato juice, black pepper and Tabasco to taste. Serve in shot glasses as tequila chasers or mix the two for a fabulous Bloody Maria.

40% vol; www.ochotequila.com

"SOBER OR BLOTTO,
THIS IS YOUR MOTTO:
KEEP MUDDLING THROUGH."

P.G. WODEHOUSE,
A DAMSEL IN DISTRESS

PAUL GIRAUD VSOP COGNAC FRANCE

As a thirsty punter after a fine cognac, it's all too easy to stick with what you know and to go for something reassuringly popular. Cognac is not dissimilar in this respect to Champagne: both regions are dominated by familiar, big names and they're often the easiest/best to aim for.

Producers of cognac such as Hennessy, Martell, Rémy Martin and Courvoisier make very fine spirits just as producers such as Veuve Clicquot, Pol Roger, Ruinart and Bollinger make very fine fizz in Champagne. You know where you are with them.

At the other end of the scale, with both cognac and champagne, it's best to avoid the cheap stuff. The trouble is that the term 'cognac' on a label is no more a guarantee of quality than is the term 'champagne'. All it tells you is that the spirit was twice distilled in copper pot stills and aged for at least two years in French oak barrels somewhere in Cognac. A lot of lousy brandy can claim that, and be distilled from poor-quality wine, and aged in poor-quality wood for the bare minimum. You need to be on your guard.

However, if you're feeling adventurous or you've put yourself in the hands of a merchant or sommelier you trust then there are some truly glorious cognacs to explore. This is just such a one, an absolute corker from a producer I bet you've not heard of (don't worry, nor had I until a few months ago).

Paul Giraud's family has been making first-rate cognac, father to son, since the 1650s. They only use grapes from their own, sustainably farmed vineyards in the heart of Grande Champagne. They have also been laying down reserves for decades in their cellars. The legal minimum age for VSOP cognac is four years; this is aged for eight, in seasoned, lightly toasted oak barrels. It's both light and earthy; there's honey and cream on the palate; and it's vibrantly fresh and satisfyingly fruity. It's exceptional and it proves what treasures can be found beyond the big names.

40% vol; www.cognac-paulgiraud.com

PIMM'S NO. 6 CUP ENGLAND

Ooh, I do love a large glass of Pimm's! It's the essential partner to what we still laughingly refer to in England as summer and I don't care whether it's blazing sun or sheeting rain but from late April until early September you'll never find me far away from a brimming jug of the stuff.

This magnificent concoction was invented in the 1840s by James Pimm, a proprietor of several oyster bars in London. Potent, badly made gin was his customers' tipple of choice but JP reckoned he could improve it by blending the gin with herbs, spices and caramelized orange and then sell it in a small tankard known as a 'No. 1 Cup'. He was right; he could. It was an instant success and Pimm soon flogged the oyster bars in order to concentrate on making more of what had become known as Pimm's No. 1.

These days Pimm's is owned by Diageo and it's made to the same original recipe, a secret known to just six people. The company has introduced various other fruit cups over the years, namely: No. 2 Cup (whisky-based); No. 3 (brandy-based); No. 4 (rum-based); No. 5 (rye-based) and No. 6 (vodka-based). Pimm's No. 1 has been the only constant. Pimm's No. 6 stuttered along for a while (largely because the then chairman's wife liked it) but then disappeared until its reintroduction in 2015. Pimm's No. 3 has also made a comeback as Pimm's Winter. The most recent addition is Pimm's Blackberry & Elderflower.

Pimm's No. 6 has always been my favourite. I find it slightly drier, cleaner, crisper and ultimately more refreshing than the No. 1. The classic serve of one part Pimm's to three parts lemonade comes out at about 5.4% vol, the same as most lagers. I find it much more interesting – yes, yes, I mean more alcoholic – if one sloshes in some decent Prosecco or champagne alongside the lemonade. The fizz just gives more oomph and character. And I rarely bother with all the vegetation that many like to add. A sprig of mint and some ice is enough for me. Oh and if possible, some sunshine.

25% vol; www.anyoneforpimms.com

QUAGLIA APERITIVO BÈRTO ITALY

One sip of this and I was completely besotted. I can't remember when I last had a drink hitherto unknown to me that bowled me over quite so comprehensively.

It was early evening and I was in a bar in Parma with English friends and we were just marvelling at how well the Italians do this aperitivo thing. Where we Brits seem easily satisfied with a pint of warm ale or glass of Prosecco in the Dog and Vomit on the way home, Italians seem to hang out in achingly cool bars picking at tasty little morsels of food whilst being served elegant spritzes, shots and cocktails by gorgeous-looking, trendy young staff. Even the labels on the bottles look effortlessly chic.

I was dithering about what to drink as usual and whilst my chums each had a Negroni I couldn't decide and so asked the barman to choose something for me. I always excuse my habitual indecision by telling myself that this is a great way to discover new drinks when on unfamiliar territory.

Anyway Quaglia Aperitivo Bèrto was the recommendation and, as I say, one sip and I was a goner. It has everything I look for in an aperitivo. It just seems to bring a smile to the lips, a spring to the step and a glint to the eye. All hail, then, to the Antica Distilleria Quaglia, a 130-year-old, family-run producer of fine spirits and liqueurs in Castelnuovo Don Bosco – not far from Turin – which produces this nectar.

It's deliciously creamy in texture, rich and both bitter and sweet, rather like Seville orange marmalade, with noticeable hints of rhubarb, ginger and spice. I'm told there's also gentian root in it, along with several other herbs and botanicals. It knocks spots off such aperitivos as the violently hued Aperol and makes a far, far better spritz. It teed me up just so, that night in Parma, and now that I've found where to get it in the UK, it's become standard teeing-up fare at home.

15% vol; www.distilleriaquaglia.it

RAMSBURY SINGLE ESTATE VODKA
ENGLAND

This very fine English vodka comes from the heart of Wiltshire and the proud boast is that whatever they needed to make it – be it the wheat or the chalk-filtered water – originates from the Ramsbury Estate surrounding the distillery.

The property is owned by squillionaire Stefan Persson, the proprietor of the H&M retail clothing company, and, being Swedish, one imagines that he knows more than a little about vodka. Not that he can have much time on his hands for such fripperies as tasting vodka. After all, he not only has H&M to run but presumably the 19,000 acres of northeast Wiltshire, west Berkshire and north Hampshire and the brewery, the smokehouse (which smokes estate-reared game, trout and bacon) and the seventeenth-century pub (The Bell – recently voted AA Pub of the Year) that comprise Ramsbury Estate need a bit of attention too.

The distillery and brewery are heated by wood from the estate's forest and the livestock are fed brewers' grains and it's all as sustainable, self-supporting and ethical a set up as you will find. And do you know what? I rather like the fact that the label tells me what wheat is used (Horatio); which farm it was grown on (Stockclose Farm in Wiltshire); in which field (Middle Furlong – they even give the map reference); and when it was planted (September 2014), harvested (August 2015) and distilled (autumn 2015).

Everyone now loves to buy local and loves to know the provenance of what they're eating and drinking and given that vodka – on the whole – doesn't have a lot to say about itself, all this info rather pleases me and makes a shot of Ramsbury vodka a talking point if nothing else. Luckily, it's also a bloody good vodka – creamy and fresh with more than a hint of citrus – and the quince-influenced gin they make is tip-top too. One day I'll get round to trying their beer.

43% vol; www.ramsbury.com

123

THE BLOODY MARY

Where would we be without the Bloody Mary? I mean, where would we be?! I'll tell you. Lost and adrift on a sea of misery, that's where we'd be.

The Bloody Mary is without equal. It's able to stand in for any meal of the day, nourishing you in a way that no other cocktail can (just think of all that vitamin C, vitamin B6, vitamin E, niacin and dietary fibre); it lifts you up and fortifies you when you're feeling down; and it restores the equilibrium after a night on the tiles when the idea of solids or even a cheering Buck's Fizz makes you shudder. No other cocktail can repair the damage or at least paper over the cracks better than a Bloody Mary.

Fernand Petiot is usually credited as the creator of this panacea, the date given for his invention varying from 1921, when he worked at Harry's Bar, Paris, to 1934, by which time he was head barman at the St Regis Hotel, New York. Others, though, claim that it was actor George Jessel who came up with the idea of mixing vodka with tomato juice in 1939, and that it was Petiot who made it the more elaborate creation we know today by adding all the other tasty bits.

Well, bless them both I say, since a finely crafted, lovingly served BM is nothing if not life-enhancing. A word of caution: it needs to be a good one, since a bad one can be very bad indeed.

Woe betide anyone, for example, who orders a Bloody Mary on a plane or train. Only the other day, like an idiot, I ordered a BM on a flight and had slammed down on my table the bare minimum of a tin of warm tomato juice, a miniature vodka and a cube of ice in a plastic cup. My request for some Lea & Perrins Worcestershire sauce, lemon and Tabasco got a wordless stare.

'Why do you always do this to yourself?' sighed my ever-loving wife, Marina. 'You knew what was coming and you're now needlessly upset and cross. Stop baiting them, have a glass of wine like everyone else and grow up.' Hrrrmph.

Everyone considers their own recipe the best, of course, and invariably strives to add their own little twist. Some add horseradish, say, some add sweet paprika, some add chilli flakes and some – like the late, great Kingsley Amis – add tomato ketchup.

I keep my recipe relatively simple and, although I say it myself, it's a belter. You need good vodka (it's only there to give the kick of alcohol and a bit of texture) and you need outstanding tomato juice. Ketel One Citroen Vodka (page 96) works perfectly thanks to its citrus notes, as does Ramsbury Single Estate Vodka (page 123), too, thanks to its creamy quality.

As for the tomato juice, well, I've not been bribed or paid to say this but will be failing in my duty if I didn't tell you that the finest in all the world comes from the Tomato Stall on the Isle of Wight. It's made only from the freshest squished tomatoes with no added citric acid, salt or anything. It's sweeter, richer, juicier and less acidic than the usual dreary stuff in the supermarkets and I can't recommend it highly enough. Visit www.thetomatostall.co.uk and see for yourself.

I mix vodka, tomato juice, dry sherry (La Gitana or Tio Pepe for choice), freshly squeezed lemon juice, freshly squeezed orange juice, Lea & Perrins Worcestershire sauce, Tabasco, pepper and celery salt in a big jug and keep in the fridge until really cold.

I sometimes add some fresh chives, basil or coriander (cilantro). I never put ice in the glass as this just dilutes the carefully crafted mixture. And I don't bother with set measurements either since sometimes I fancy it with more of a sherry note and sometimes with a bit more orange. I simply adjust to taste.

A little stick of celery in the glass works perfectly as a stirrer and something to munch on, and if I or my guests are really peckish I also add a rasher of crispy bacon too.

Some folk like to substitute gin for vodka, in which case the drink becomes a Red Snapper, and some tequila or mezcal. I think this is all a bit outré. I do occasionally add some melted gelatine, though, and pour into moulds to make Bloody Mary jelly, than which there is no finer opener to a long, rambling Sunday lunch.

REGAL ROGUE WILD ROSÉ VERMOUTH
AUSTRALIA

At the time of writing, the aperitivo of the day in my favourite local restaurant – Cin Cin, an exquisite taste of Italy in Brighton's North Laine – is a Regal Rogue Wild Rosé Vermouth and Sicilian lemonade. It's so simple and so tasty and it's almost impossible to stick to just the one. Not for nothing is this Regal Rogue marketed as the world's first quaffing vermouth.

I must also point out that Fabrizio at Cin Cin is very persuasive. And as for Mrs Ray, well, she's a bloody pushover. She's also half Australian and given that Regal Rogue is 100 per cent Australian she feels she's simply doing her bit for the land down under by demanding a second glass.

It's hard not to be seduced by Regal Rogue, by the beautiful paper-wrapped bottles with their jaunty knight in armour on the front and – more importantly – by the liquid inside.

There are four vermouths in the range: the Lively White, the Bold Red, the Daring Dry and this, the Wild Rosé. They are all exceptionally well made, in small batches, based on fine Australian vino enhanced with native botanicals. The Wild Rosé has a juicy Barossa Valley Shiraz Rosé at its heart, lifted by some strawberry gum, rosella and Illawarra plum aromatics. I love it as a spritzer mixed with a splash of Aperol and topped up with a fine Prosecco although the aforementioned serve at Cin Cin is hard to beat. Simply slosh 50ml (1¾fl oz) Wild Rosé into a glass and top up with really good lemonade and some ice.

It's perfect for swigging at as you pick at a plate of venison bresaola and Parmesan or guanciale and Sicilian flat bread.

16.5% vol; www.regalrogue.com

"THE FIRST QUIET DRINK OF THE EVENING IN A QUIET BAR – THAT'S WONDERFUL."

RAYMOND CHANDLER,
THE LONG GOODBYE

ST-GERMAIN ELDERFLOWER LIQUEUR
FRANCE

Have you ever tried this? You haven't?! Oh my goodness you've a treat in store, then, because it's staggeringly, swooningly, tongue-teasingly delicious.

You will have seen the gorgeous bottle (which I say is Art Nouveau and Mrs Ray says is Art Deco) on the back bar of some fine hostelry I'm sure and if you really haven't tried it I'm afraid I must insist that you do so immediately. I mean, like this very minute. You will thank me, I promise. Just slosh a decent measure into a chilled champagne flute and top up with fine ice-cold fizz. Pop a strawberry in too if you feel frivolous, or a lemon twist. Mmm, mmmm!

So elegant, so chic and so retro is the bottle in its fin de siècle-like way (according to me) that I assumed that it had been around forever, fuelling the creative juices of Lautrec, Mucha, Verlaine and the like in the bistros, brasseries and bordellos of late nineteenth-century Paris. But no, it was created in 2007 by the distilling wunderkind that was the late Robert J. Cooper, who died suddenly – sadly young – in 2016.

It's made in France by resolutely artisanal methods. Elderflower blossom is collected by hand by scores of independent pickers during the brief flowering period in late spring. The blossom, which is often delivered by pickers on specially adapted bicycles, is weighed (pickers are paid by the kilo) and then macerated immediately in order to retain freshness.

They use a unique, secret method of maceration after they discovered that simply pressing the flowers led to an unpleasant bitterness; that freezing them led to a loss of complexity; and that traditional maceration gave little in the way of flavour. The elderflower maceration is then married to grape spirit and a pure cane sugar solution.

The result is stunning. It smells headily of elderflower, of course, but also of honeysuckle, lychee and citrus. It's supremely refreshing when added to a G&T, say, a Gimlet, French 75 or an Old Fashioned. Indeed, so successful is St-Germain in enhancing traditional and novel cocktails that it's often referred to as 'bartenders' ketchup'.

20% vol; www.stgermain.fr

"I'D RATHER HAVE A BOTTLE IN FRONT OF ME THAN A FRONTAL LOBOTOMY."

DOROTHY PARKER

SANTA TERESA 1796 RUM
VENEZUELA

The Santa Teresa plantation is some 50 kilometres (30 miles) southwest of Caracas, near the village of El Consejo in the municipality of Revenga. The family-owned estate dates from 1796 and the distillery from 1884. Oh, and the rugby pitch dates from 2003. Yes, a rugby pitch: in the wilds of Venezuela. It's just one of the many things that make these people, this place, this distillery and this rum so darn special.

Santa Teresa 1796, the estate's flagship rum, is what it is thanks to the solera system. Casks of rum are stacked in tiers with the oldest rums at the bottom and the youngest at the top. Rums from the bottom tier are partially drawn off and the casks topped up with rums from the tier above which are then themselves topped up from the tier above and so on. This is how the Spanish make sherry, the Portuguese make madeira and the Italians make Marsala. However, I can't think of many other rums made this way.

The result is spectacular. Santa Teresa 1796 is sweet and fruity on the nose with hints of leather, vanilla, maple syrup, spice and bitter chocolate. It's velvety soft in the mouth and although light and delicate, it's blessed with the longest of finishes. Drink it neat or with a cube of ice or simply with a splash of sparkling mineral water. You will love it!

But back to that rugby pitch. Alberto Vollmer, who along with his brother Enrique and four sisters represents the fifth generation of his family to own this estate, fell in love with rugby whilst a student in France in the 1980s. He realized there was a place for the game here and through Santa Teresa's extraordinary social integration initiative known as Project Alcatraz, he introduced rugby to the violent criminal gangs of Revenga with astonishingly successful results. Suffice to say that there were 114 murders per 100,000 inhabitants in Revenga in 2003, the year rugby was introduced; in 2013 there were 12. Google the story: it's fascinating.

40% vol; www.ronsantateresa.com

1615 PISCO PURO ITALIA PERU

Just what is it about pisco that makes you think that another one is always a good idea, even when your legs have already waved goodbye to your brain? Well I'm the last person to ask. All I know is that this example is absolutely perfect for making a fine Pisco Sour and I defy you not to have a second – or even a third. And that of course is where your troubles will begin.

Pisco is the name given in both Chile and Peru to brandy distilled from fermented grape juice. It originated with the Spanish conquerors in the sixteenth century and is now big business. But when I say brandy, it's not like cognac or armagnac – rounded, mellow and amber-coloured, after time spent in oak. Pisco is different.

The name derives from the port city and province of Pisco, Peru, although when I was last in Chile a pisco producer told me that the word means 'high flying bird' which, he insisted, is what drinkers imagined they were after too many glasses...

Bodega San Nicolás, some 250 kilometres (155 miles) south of Lima, only uses the fruit from their own vineyards to make their pisco and their 1615 range is named after the year in which grapes were first cultivated in the area. Grapes are picked in March, deseeded and then pressed to give a pure juice. This is fermented and then distilled in copper pot stills after which it rests for up to six months. And that's it. Neither sugar nor water is added and no time is spent in oak.

And because pisco is so unadulterated, you can actually taste which grape it's made from. Pisco Puro means that it's made from just one variety, in this instance the fragrant and juicy Italia, a table grape in Europe but one of four aromatic varieties permitted in Peruvian pisco. Acholado means it's a blend. You'll love it. You can sip it neat of course, but it really cries out to be made into a Pisco Sour by simply adding lime juice, sugar syrup, Angostura Bitters and egg white. Perfecto!

40% vol; www.pisco1615.pe

131

SOMERSET CIDER BRANDY 10 YEAR OLD
ENGLAND

What little I remember of my visit to Pass Vale Farm is this: it's somewhere in Somerset, it's rather pretty in a *Darling Buds of May* sort of way, the cider they make is really very fine and the cider brandy even better.

Oh and that when I called my wife to assure her that I was on the next train home, proprietor Julian Temperley promptly opened another bottle. And that when I called her again to say I'd missed said train, he opened another. And that this process was repeated, I think, four times before Mrs Ray put her foot down and roared, 'For God's sake, grow up!' down the phone and off, finally, I had to scuttle.

Forty different varieties of apple are grown here – such as Kingston Black, Dabinett, Stoke Red, Yarlington Mill and Harry Masters – in 150 acres (60 hectares) of orchards, and about 1,000 tons of fruit are pressed a year.

Temperley's prize-winning ciders are greatly sought after (especially at festivals such as Glastonbury thanks to his notorious Cider Bus) but it's his Somerset Cider Brandy that has had folk in raptures, ever since he was granted the UK's first full cider-distilling licence by HM Customs, in 1989.

Apples are gathered in the autumn, blended and pressed. The juice is fermented in huge oak vats and after three months the resulting cider is distilled in one of two elderly French continuous stills – Josephine or Fifi. The spirit is then put into old sherry casks, or new oak barrels from Hungary or France, with the results being bottled at three, five, ten, 15 and 20 years old.

And don't go thinking these are just carbon copies of calvados either. As Temperley points out, Somerset and Normandy have different soil, climate, apples and barrels and Somerset Cider Brandy is as different from calvados as bordeaux wine is from burgundy.

Make no mistake, these brandies are utterly stunning. If I had to choose a favourite it would be this, the 10 Year Old. Why? Because it's the bottle that JT quietly slipped into my hand to enjoy on that last train home.

42% vol; www.somersetciderbrandy.com

"EVERYTHING IN MODERATION, INCLUDING MODERATION."

OSCAR WILDE

SOUTHERN COMFORT 100 PROOF USA

Southern Comfort has changed a bit over the years. When I was growing up it was deemed to be rather cool in a Jack Daniel's sort of way, beloved of rockers, would-be rockers and whiskey lovers. More recently, however, I get the sense that one day it woke up to find itself filed under N for 'naff', whilst JD remained resolutely hip.

And from what I gather, the recipe has changed a bit too. When it was created in 1874 by one Martin Wilkes Heron, a bartender in New Orleans (his embossed signature remains on the bottle to this day), the fruit- and spice-based liqueur had whiskey at its heart, whereas during the years of Brown-Forman's ownership I understand that the whiskey was largely replaced with neutral grain spirit. Not that most people seemed to notice or care.

Southern Comfort was bought from Brown-Forman in 2016 by the Sazerac Company (along with the fabled Tuaca – see page 144) and I'm told that whiskey is firmly back at the core of the recipe and that they're making every effort to make it cool again and to appeal to whiskey lovers. I've always rather liked the stuff and remember feeling very devil-may-care and Keith Richards-like when I drank it at university. The key, when taking it to parties, was to swig it casually from the bottle – which you held by the neck – and to lope around bow-leggedly and loose-hipped rather than walk. Nobody took a blind bit of notice but I felt rather cool.

The front label calls Southern Comfort 'The Spirit of New Orleans' whereas the back label (in rather smaller letters) explains that it's produced in Europe (I'm not sure where). No matter, because the Southern Comfort 100 Proof is really very potable. It has more oomph than the original without losing those typical sweet/spicy/orange notes. It's also great in cocktails such as the Alabama Slammer, the Slow Comfortable Screw Against the Wall and the Scarlett O'Hara. Just don't go calling it the SoCo. That's irredeemably naff.

50% vol; www.southerncomfort.com

SPIRIT OF HVEN ORGANIC SUMMER SPIRIT SWEDEN

I really can't work out which I prefer: the Spirit of Hven Summer Spirit or the Spirit of Hven Winter Spirit. And there's no point telling me to have the one in the summer and the other in the winter because an English summer is pretty much akin to everyone else's winter and an English winter is, well, too damp, dark and depressing, although perhaps not quite so damp, dark and depressing as a Swedish one. Ok, I'll flip a coin... Ah, there we are: Spirit of Hven Summer Spirit it is.

The island of Hven lies in the strait of Øresund, between the southernmost tip of Sweden and the Danish island of Zealand and it's home to no more than 350 people. Of much more importance to us browsers and sluicers, though, is that it's also home to the Spirit of Hven Distillery, founded in 2008 as part of a hotel and conference centre. They make excellent single malt whisky here as well as gin, vodka and akvavit. What I enjoy most, though, are their two seasonal spirits – effectively flavoured vodkas – which are both so delicious and unlike anything else you will have tasted.

Both spirits are distilled in small copper pot stills from organic wheat and then matured for a period in American oak. The Spirit of Winter is made with cinnamon, cloves and oranges and the Spirit of Summer is made with elderflower, apple, rhubarb, orange bitters and various local foraged botanicals (all organic) and both are aged again in American oak. Both spirits evoke their nominal seasons: the Spirit of Summer is apple-fresh, rhubarby and zesty with hints of wild summer herbs, and the Spirit of Winter is mellow and spicy and reminds me of freshly made plum pudding cooling on a plate.

I reckon both are best served on their own on the rocks or with some decent sparkling wine, with one-third Spirit of Summer/Winter to two-thirds fizz. Enjoy and don't worry about what the bloody weather's doing.

38% vol; www.hven.com

135

STAGG JR KENTUCKY STRAIGHT BOURBON WHISKEY USA

Stagg Jr is one of many fine whiskies made at Buffalo Trace Distillery in Frankfort, capital of the Commonwealth of Kentucky. The distillery, so-named because it stands on an ancient buffalo migration route, has been in continuous use for well over 200 years, longer than any other distillery in America, and it's responsible for one heck of a lot of whiskey.

They produce such celebrated brands as Van Winkle, Elmer T. Lee, Sazerac Rye, Eagle Rare, and in early 2018 Buffalo Trace celebrated the production of its seven millionth barrel since the end of Prohibition in 1933. Not that the distillery can have been much bothered by Prohibition given that – uniquely – it was given special permission to keep distilling 'for medicinal purposes'. Apparently, doctors were able to prescribe patients a pint of bourbon every ten days for various trifling ailments and by the time Prohibition ended in 1933 quacks had written a total of six million prescriptions. 'Two spoonfuls in hot water and sugar to be taken three times daily,' said the note from 1925 that I spotted on display at Buffalo Trace. Now that's just the sort of medical advice I take seriously.

And as far as I know they could still be issuing such instructions given that around a third of Kentucky is still 'dry' (including – I kid you not – Bourbon County, which gave the local whiskey its name in the first place).

Stagg Jr would certainly make a fine medicine and a mighty punchy one, too, given that it's a whopping 65% vol. It won the Gold Medal at the 2017 International Spirits Challenge and is as big and as bold as they come. It's bottled unfiltered and is fabulously complex with rich, dark chocolate notes, candied orange peel, raisins, toffee, vanilla and buckets of sweet spice. It is almost too overwhelming and even though I'm hard as nails and always take my medicine like a man, I invariably give in and add a liver-friendly splash of water.

65% vol; www.buffalotracedistillery.com

THE STORY GIN AUSTRALIA

When I last visited Melbourne, I timed it perfectly. I arrived just as the city's Food and Wine Festival was kicking off and if there's a better cure for jetlag than heading to Southgate Plaza and getting stuck into the scores of wine stalls set up along the banks of the Yarra River then I'd like to know about it, please. There was one heck of a buzz and a distinct shortage of spittoons and I soon realized that it was more a vast public drinks party than a wine tasting. The Aussies looked bronzed, healthy, happy and, well, just a little sozzled. And so, adopting the principle of when in Rome... I dived in.

I've always loved the wines of Victoria – the silky Pinot Noirs from Mornington Peninsula; the Italian varieties of King Valley; the fortified wines of Rutherglen; the fizzes of Yarra Valley – and I drank my fill that day.

One of Victoria's quirkiest producers is The Story Wines, based not amid rolling hills and vineyards, but in a drab (their word) suburb of Melbourne without a vine in sight. They're part of the new trend for urban wineries that truck in fruit from vineyards in the Grampians and Henty and vinify and mature the wines in the city. And it works a treat, for the wines – particularly their Rieslings and Shirazes – are fabulous. Their labels are fabulous, too, not least because of the 800-word short stories they print on them as part of their Story Wine Prize initiative.

The wackiest of all labels, though, is that of the new small-batch gin that winemaker Rory Lane makes in partnership with his mates at Gypsy Brewing. It's in handwritten print with a little note for those in doubt stressing that THIS IS NOT WINE. And bloody good not wine it is too, made using native Australian botanicals such as finger lime, lemon myrtle, mountain pepper berry, wattle seed, lemon scented gum and so on. It's bottled unfiltered and is deliciously citrusy and spicy with a distinct scent of the Australian bush. It's as Aussie as they come and absolutely ripper.

42% vol; www.thestory.com.au

TALISKER SKYE SINGLE MALT SCOTCH WHISKY SCOTLAND

Talisker, established in 1830 in the village of Carbost on the Isle of Skye is dramatically sited slap bang on the shore of Loch Harport. It's a rugged spot and no mistake. There is a safe anchorage here for stout-hearted yachties, although getting to and from it can be interesting if it's blowing a gale.

I spent a very jolly few days on the island a year or so ago. The weather was utterly vile until the minute it was time to leave when, of course, the sun came out in all its glory and the wind dropped to a mere zephyr. I've never seen a sea calmer than it was during the ferry ride between Armadale and Mallaig that day. It was as flat as, well, the flattest of snooker tables.

Whilst on Skye I stayed at the Toravaig House Hotel and divided my time between stuffing my face there in the Iona Restaurant and in The Three Chimneys (*The Good Food Guide*'s Restaurant of the Year 2018) at the other end of the island, and being blown this way and that as I hiked in the Cuillin Hills and scrambled up and down the Old Man of Storr. What I did most of, though, was sit by the fire and drink buckets of Talisker. I've always loved Talisker and there's invariably a bottle of 10 Year Old at home. With its sweet, peppery spiciness, touch of citrus and lightest of light peat notes, it's just so drinkable and uncomplicated. I really enjoy the slightly fruitier and sweeter 18 Year Old too. My new favourite, though, is this, the Talisker Skye, launched in 2015.

It has that same Talisker accessibility, of course, but there's something extra, maybe a touch more smokiness or maybe sweetness. Or maybe it's slightly saltier. I don't know, there's just a bit more depth and complexity to it. And I'll tell you something for nothing, it goes beautifully with salted caramel chocolate. Sip the whisky first and then let the chocolate melt in your mouth and wonder why you've never done it before.

45.8% vol; www.malts.com

TANQUERAY NO. TEN GIN SCOTLAND

My old friend Malcolm – sadly no longer with us – loved Tanqueray No. Ten. It was his favourite of all gins and he reckoned he could spot it in a glass at twenty paces. Malcolm was head of the wine committee at a very swanky home counties golf club and I'm sure he'd not mind me telling you of the time that his supposedly infallible nose for Tanq Ten let him down. He used to tell the story against himself in any case.

One Sunday, after a morning on the course, Malcolm foolishly had two or three large G&Ts in the bar before heading home. He got into his Jag and, on turning out of the drive rather faster than was prudent, had the misfortune to be spotted by a police car. He was pulled over and invited to blow into a breathalyser. Being a gent, Malcolm fessed up and said there was no need for him to do so because he'd had several G&Ts and would be over the limit. The police thanked him for his honesty and explained that they had to follow procedure. He blew into the bag and – guess what? – passed. When asked to try again with another machine, he passed again. The police thanked him for his time, warned him about his speed and waved him on his way. Malcolm headed straight back to the club where he promptly sacked the barman for watering down the gin. He was outraged.

Tanqueray No. Ten is so named because it was first developed by a Charles Tanqueray in the 1830s and – now owned by Diageo – is produced in small batches in still No. 10, known as 'Tiny Ten'.

Juniper, coriander, liquorice and angelica form the gin's backbone, with lighter notes provided by fresh whole citrus fruits and camomile flowers. It's quadruple distilled and is exceptionally smooth. It's a marvellous all-rounder and works in all manner of cocktails thanks to its intense citrus notes, its bold juniper character and its hearty strength, the lack of which in his G&T poor Malcolm should have spotted.

47.3% vol; www.tanqueray.com

MY TEN FAVOURITE COCKTAIL BARS

Everyone has a favourite cocktail bar. It might be one's favourite because of where it is – comfortingly local or exotically far-flung – or it might be one's favourite because of its sublime cocktails, its warm welcome, its fame or – indeed – its anonymity. It might be one's favourite simply because of whom one goes there with.

These, alphabetically, are my favourite bars. I'm fickle, though, and they're only my favourites at the moment. I could easily have found another two or three by next Tuesday. Until I do, though, these are they. I don't claim that they are the best in the world (although several of them unquestionably are); no, they are simply my current favourites for any or all of the above reasons.

ARTESIAN BAR, LONDON, UK
www.artesian-bar.co.uk

The Artesian has been voted Best Bar in the World a ridiculous number of times. Gaze at its glorious pagoda-like back bar, count the astonishing number of rums and hug yourself with delight.

LE BAR DU BRISTOL, PARIS, FRANCE
www.oetkercollection.com/destinations/le-bristol-paris

A sumptuously sophisticated spot this, in a famously fine hotel. That all-time classic, the Old Fashioned, is taken to new quirky heights here with popcorn syrup, bitter orange and mandarin.

BARCHEF, TORONTO, CANADA
www.barcheftoronto.com

The cocktails here are as exciting to look at, touch, smell and – occasionally – listen to as they are to taste. The Spring Thaw (for example) comes in a dry-ice-shrouded mini garden of moss and foraged herbs.

BEMELMANS BAR, NEW YORK, USA
www.rosewoodhotels.com/en/the-carlyle-new-york/dining/bemelmans-bar

A chic, Manhattan legend set in The Carlyle Hotel. Sit at the stunning black granite bar and kick off with a Valencia – gin, sherry and orange oil, served with flaming orange peel.

CAHOOTS, LONDON, UK
www.cahoots-london.com

Down some steps just off Carnaby Street, a 'disused' 1940s Underground station complete with Tube carriage, sandbags and jazz/swing music. Both conceit and cocktails are tip-top.

THE DEAD RABBIT GROCERY AND GROG, NEW YORK, USA
www.deadrabbitnyc.com

Belfast bad boys Jack McGarry and Sean Muldoon famously took NYC by storm with their gritty take on mixology and The Dead Rabbit has been a worthy Best Bar in the World in both 2015 and 2016.

EXPERIMENTAL COCKTAIL CLUB, PARIS, FRANCE
www.experimentalcocktail.club.com

A deliciously decadent speakeasy-style bar in the heart of Paris, it has been delighting both locals and visitors alike for over a decade. It started the Parisian cocktail revolution and remains the best.

MOSKOVSKY BAR, MOSCOW, RUSSIA
www.fourseasons.com/moscow

You must come here if only for the Moskovsky Mule made with vodka, ginger beer, honey, limes, cloves, cumin and cinnamon served over a nugget of ice cut from Siberia's Lake Baikal.

SUNSHINE'S BAR AND GRILL, SAINT KITTS AND NEVIS, LEEWARD ISLANDS
www.sunshinesbeachrestaurantsnapshot.com

Not so much a cocktail bar as a sprawling shack on Pinney's Beach, Nevis, and famous the world over as home to the high-octane Killer Bee cocktail. One is never nearly enough and two are way too many.

28 HONG KONG STREET, SINGAPORE
www.28hks.com

Behind an anonymous door in an anonymous street, it's mighty hard to find. Thanks to its darkly lit, intimate interior, lovingly made classic and innovative creations, it's mighty hard to leave.

"AFTER THE FIRST GLASS, YOU SEE THINGS AS YOU WISH THEY WERE. AFTER THE SECOND, YOU SEE THINGS AS THEY ARE NOT. FINALLY, YOU SEE THINGS AS THEY REALLY ARE, AND THAT IS THE MOST HORRIBLE THING IN THE WORLD."

OSCAR WILDE

TAPATIO AÑEJO TEQUILA MEXICO

Like many folk my age – pushing 60, since you ask, and don't you dare rub it in – my first exposure to tequila was via that emblematic and really rather sickly cocktail of the seventies, the Tequila Sunrise. You know the one I mean, where you get a highball glass and carefully pour in tequila, then ice, then orange juice and finally grenadine, so that the colours don't mix but remained layered and thus resemble, well, a rather cheesy sunrise. My mates and I would blag our way into Trader Vic's under the Hilton Hotel in London's Park Lane and reckoned we were quite 'the thing' as we preened and puffed and eyed the girls. We didn't much like the cocktail, though, but pretended to each other that we did.

Having made one the other day just to remind myself, I realize I still don't. It's too sweet. And that's part of the problem: Tequila Sunrise back then was invariably made with cheap, sweetened tequila, not gorgeous aged tequila like this, which is far too good to use so basely.

As you know, tequila is made in Mexico (mainly in the state of Jalisco) from the blue agave plant, a cactus lookalike but a relative of the lily, apparently. Its stiff, sharp leaves are removed by hand by farmers known as *jimadores*, leaving the heart of the plant (the *piña*), which is then steamed in brick ovens to convert starches to sugars. The cooked agave is passed through a mill, extracting all the sugars from the fibres, resulting in a sweet, rich 'honey water' or *aguamiel*; this is fermented with yeast and distilled into tequila.

Like a lot of fine tequila brands this aged example (18 months in old bourbon barrels – far longer than the legal requirement) comes from La Alteña Distillery, home also to the excellent Ocho (see page 117). It's full flavoured and fruity and surprisingly creamy. There's a touch of spice, some sweetness and a gentle suggestion of herbs. It deserves to be sipped and savoured rather than just sloshed into a crappy Tequila Sunrise. You'll thank me.

38% vol; www.tequilatapatio.mx

TUACA ITALY

What? You haven't heard of Tuaca? Well, you clearly
don't live in or visit Brighton then. I'm told that something
approaching 95 per cent of all Tuaca sales in the UK are
in Brighton and there isn't a bar, club, hotel, restaurant or
corner shop there that doesn't stock it.

Brighton is my hometown and it's fair to say that I've drunk
more than my fair share of Tuaca (pronounced: twacker).
In truth, I'm not even really that keen on it. I only include it
in these pages because no night out in Brighton is complete
without a last minute shot or so of Tuaca. You know the
score: it's chucking out time, you glance at your mates and
all of you think and one of you actually says: 'Right, shall
we all have just one Tuaca for the road?' You sink one each,
the barman stands you all another and next thing you know
you're at Grubb's getting a late night burger before hailing
a cab to take you to the Pink Coconut or worse. As Mrs Ray
keeps telling me, it's not big and it's not clever.

Tuaca's original recipe is said to have been created in
Renaissance Italy expressly for Lorenzo the Magnificent. It was
rediscovered in the 1930s by brothers-in-law Gaetano Tuoni
and Giorgio Canepa who named it Tuoca as a play on their
surnames and, later, Tuaca.

It became popular in Brighton thanks to the fact that the
owner of the St. James's Tavern discovered it on holiday in
Italy and brought a couple of cases back as part of a very
complicated bet. In no time at all it had conquered the town
and today a rather faded blue plaque hangs outside the pub
marking its role in the drink's success.

A blend of brandy, citrus and vanilla, Tuaca is soft, mellow
and approachable. It's also incredibly sweet which might
explain its popularity at night's end. I've never really noticed
this before and then realized with a shock that until I came to
write this page I'd never approached a glass of Tuaca sober.

35% vol; www.tuaca.com

VERSINTHE LA BLANCHE ABSINTHE
FRANCE

If there's one spirit that brings one era and one city to mind, it's absinthe, which – for me – instantly conjures up fin-de-siècle Paris. One sip and Offenbach's 'Infernal Galop' (the 'Can-Can' to you and me) throbs in my head, not to mention that weird snippet of 'The Hills Are Alive' from Baz Luhrmann's *Moulin Rouge*. You remember that scene where Ewan McGregor first tastes absinthe and sees the little green fairy played by Kylie Minogue, right? Of course you do.

It also reminds me of a jolly tale that the late, great Simon Hoggart – my impossible-to-follow predecessor at the *Spectator* – once told me. I'm sure he said it was about Lord Brougham and Vaux, Lord Chancellor in the 1830s, although, having checked, it seems he didn't have a son, a fact upon which the story relies. Anyway, let's imagine he did or maybe it was a later Lord Brougham. So, there was Lord B's son and heir cavorting around Paris, hitting the night spots and necking rather too much absinthe in the company of a French actress twice his age. His lordship took a dim view of this and wrote to his son, saying, 'If you don't stop seeing that wretched woman, I'll cut your allowance.' To which his son replied, 'If you don't double it, I'll marry her.'

Absinthe was famously banned in France for almost a century and was brought back to life in this instance by Liquoristerie de Provence in 1999. A selection of over 20 herbs and plants – including wormwood, star anise, sweet fennel and the like – are dried, macerated in alcohol, pressed and blended before being distilled at low temperature in a vacuum still. The result is a fine white absinthe (most are green), sweet (despite no sugar being added), herbal and full of anise/liquorice. Use it to make decadent cocktails or drink it like they used to, flambéed in a liqueur glass or by slowly dripping water onto a sugar cube and thence, via a slotted spoon, into the absinthe. Humming some Offenbach at this point is permissible.

55% vol; www.liquoristerie-provence.fr

WESTLAND SHERRY WOOD AMERICAN SINGLE MALT WHISKEY USA

It had all started so well. My flight into Seattle, Washington, had landed early, security was a breeze and in no time I was checking into the Edgewater Hotel on Elliott Bay. Fans of Led Zeppelin and the bizarre will certainly know the place I mean. I spent the afternoon at the Seattle Art Museum and the Seattle Center, taking in the Space Needle, the Museum of Pop Culture and the remarkable Chihuly Garden and Glass. Then it was off to the foodies' heaven that is Pike Place Market. Dinner at Matt's in the Market was a delight: Dungeness crab and prime New York strip steak, washed down with stunning local Rhône-style wines from Rôtie Cellars.

By now I was ready for some post-prandials at The Nest, the rooftop bar of the Thompson hotel about which I'd heard so much. Except that the buggers wouldn't let me in. They bloody well barred me. Why? Because I had no bloody ID, that's why. No bloody ID? I'm 58 for heaven's sake. The last time I was barred from a club was the Café des Artistes, Fulham Road, 1976. It was ridiculous and I was seething. A sympathetic voice suggested I try the bar of the Hotel Monaco a few blocks away. This I did and I told the barman there my sorry tale. He told me I'd come to the right place and did I like whiskey? Yes, I said, especially large ones. This is what he poured me. It was dazzling. Suddenly things were looking up again.

Westland Distillery is in SoDo (South of Downtown), Seattle, home also to a number of very fine urban wineries. Westland makes terroir-driven craft whiskeys of real style. The critics love them and so, now, do I. I tried many in the range that night and this was the standout. Matured in old oloroso and PX sherry casks, it's deliciously sweet and succulent with notes of maple syrup, sweetcorn and toffee. I wasn't in the least surprised to hear that it won the Chairman's Trophy at the 2018 Ultimate Spirits Challenge.

46% vol; www.westlanddistillery.com

WYNAND FOCKINK CITROEN LIKEUR
HOLLAND

I don't know about you but I adore Amsterdam. It's one of my favourite cities. There's always something wonderful to see and do. The Van Gogh Museum and the recently refurbished Rijksmuseum are worth the trip alone. But then so is simply grabbing a bicycle from Mike's Bikes in Kerkstraat and having a gentle spin around the canals.

It's a haven for drink-lovers too. I love the beer, of course, and the speakeasy bar, Door 74, with its quirky cocktails, never fails to delight. And I can't imagine anyone not enjoying the fabulously decadent high wine (as opposed to high tea) served between 3 and 6P.M. at the Dylan Hotel on Keizersgracht. Featuring a selection of four wines by the glass and four different amuses bouches, it's the perfect way of filling that awkward gap in the afternoon when you're torn between remembering what you had for lunch and dreaming about what you're going to have for dinner.

Most importantly, I always make a beeline for the Wynand Fockink tasting tavern in Pijlsteeg, just off Dam Square, unchanged since the company was founded in 1679. This wood-panelled bar with its shelves groaning with antique bottles is absurdly atmospheric and is beloved of tourists. Canny locals flock here too, though, to enjoy the widest and tastiest selection of jenevers, liqueurs and fruit brandies in all Holland.

You can buy a 'flight' of several liqueurs at a time, served in elegant tulip-shaped glasses. These are filled to the absolute brim and tradition dictates that the first sip is taken at the bar, without using one's hands.

As you might expect, the jenevers are exceptional, as traditional as they come. But it's the liqueurs and fruit brandies that draw me here time and again.

Highlights include a fierily fine ginger liqueur, a marzipan-like bitter almond liqueur, a triple sec-rivalling orange liqueur and a stunning raspberry liqueur.

This lemon liqueur, though, just edges it as my favourite of all the offerings. It's so delicate, so stylish and so zestily fresh that it knocks even the finest of limoncellos straight out of the park. I can't resist saying it: it's Fockink lovely!

28% vol; www.wynand-fockink.nl

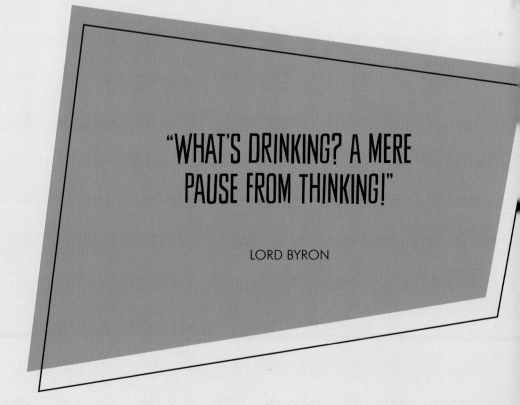

"WHAT'S DRINKING? A MERE PAUSE FROM THINKING!"

LORD BYRON

COCKTAIL RECIPES

This is a book on spirits and liqueurs rather than cocktails. But since we encounter so many of the spirits in these pages as part of a cocktail it seems only right to chuck in a few easy recipes.

I've listed in the following pages ten of the most famous of all cocktails. After all, it's vital to know the classics. Get these under your belt and then you can start to experiment. Half the fun is inventing your own and you can rustle one up in moments.

I mean, by the time you've read to the end of this paragraph you could have made a modest Peartini, say. Simply slosh some vodka, triple sec and fresh pear juice into an ice-filled Boston shaker, shake it around a bit and strain into a martini glass. And that's it! So simple and so delicious.

Or how about the deliciously refreshing, gloriously tasty and reliably crowd-pleasing Woo Woo? Simply mix 25ml (1fl oz) peach schnapps, 25ml (1fl oz) vodka and 50ml (1¾fl oz) cranberry juice in a tumbler and serve over ice. Or a Horse's Neck? This, too, takes just seconds to execute. Pour 50ml (1¾fl oz) Delamain Pale & Dry XO Cognac over ice in a highball glass. Top up with Fever Tree Ginger Ale and a couple of drops of Angostura Bitters and decorate with a zest or spiral of orange. See what I mean? You're already up, up and away.

As with cooking, use the best ingredients that you can. And as with cooking, trust your instincts and feel free to experiment. Make your cocktails how you like to drink them and however classic the cocktail or however finely honed your own creations, don't feel that you have to stick too rigidly to a recipe. If you want more of this or less of that, then that's the way to enjoy it. Just remember to keep the drink balanced.

TOP TIPS

Don't be scared of ice. The more you use, the less it will melt and dilute your cocktail.

If your cocktail demands sugar or sugar syrup, use small amounts at first. You can always add more.

In order to ensure consistency, always measure your drinks rather than attempting to free-pour them.

50ml (1¾fl oz) of any spirit, 20ml (4 tsp) lemon juice and 10ml (2 tsp) sugar syrup will give you the base for scores of cocktails, to which you can add almost anything.

"I FEEL BAD FOR PEOPLE WHO DON'T DRINK. WHEN THEY WAKE UP IN THE MORNING, THAT'S AS GOOD AS THEY'RE GOING TO FEEL ALL DAY."

FRANK SINATRA

THE OLD FASHIONED
BOURBON

Apart from the Dry Martini, the most popular cocktail served in the fabled American Bar of the Savoy Hotel in London is the Old Fashioned, first created in the 1880s in the Pendennis Club in Louisville, Kentucky. It's a formidable drink and should be an essential in your armoury. It's simple to make but it takes time and needs to be done properly.

Sugar cube
2–3 dashes of Angostura Bitters
60ml (2fl oz) bourbon
Orange zest
Triple sec (optional)

Put a sugar cube in an Old Fashioned glass or tumbler, add several drops of Angostura Bitters, the tiniest splash of water and muddle until the sugar is all dissolved. Fill the glass with ice cubes or one large round ice ball and pour in the bourbon and keep stirring. Garnish with some orange zest. If you're feeling fancy, you could also add a tiny sweetening dash of triple sec. Perfect.

THE DRY MARTINI
GIN/VODKA

The most famous of all cocktails and the most easily got wrong. Every devotee has his or her own particular way of making and serving the Dry Martini. Indeed, put a number of Dry Martini lovers in the same room and they will disagree on virtually everything. Shaken or stirred? Dry or wet? Vodka or gin? Olive or lemon? Neither or both? And just think of all the hundreds of variations!

I know I risk being shot down in flames but I'll tell you how I like to make mine. Feel free to ignore me, I won't be offended in the slightest. After all, I know I'm right.

25ml (1fl oz) top-quality dry white vermouth (Dolin for choice)
75ml (2½fl oz) top-quality gin or vodka straight from
  the freezer
Strip of lemon zest

Slosh the vermouth round and round a frozen martini glass and discard after a count of ten. Pour in the gin or vodka. Stir once and serve with a strip of lemon zest.

"ONE MARTINI IS ALL RIGHT. TWO ARE TOO MANY, AND THREE ARE NOT ENOUGH."

JAMES THURBER

THE MANHATTAN
RYE WHISKEY

The Manhattan was supposedly invented at the Manhattan
Club in New York in the 1870s and should traditionally
be made with American rye whiskey although I reckon that
you can get away with bourbon. The more reckless among
you might also care to add a splash of absinthe to your
Manhattan, thereby turning it into The Waldorf. If you use
Scotch whisky rather than rye, the drink technically becomes
a Rob Roy and there are all manner of further variations such
as the Apple Manhattan – which uses calvados instead of
whisky – and the Añejo Manhattan, which uses tequila.

60ml (2fl oz) rye whiskey or bourbon
15ml (1 tbsp) sweet red vermouth
15ml (1 tbsp) dry white vermouth
Dash of Angostura Bitters
Strip of orange zest
Cocktail cherry

Put the wet ingredients into a mixing glass and stir over ice.
Strain into a frozen martini glass or small tumbler and serve
with a strip of orange zest. I like to add a cocktail cherry too.

THE SIDECAR
COGNAC

The Sidecar is a great favourite of mine and one of the first cocktails I managed to master. Its origins are a bit confused and its creation is attributed to several different folk although it almost certainly first appeared during World War One in Paris. The recipe calls for triple sec (invariably Cointreau) although I do sometimes use Grand Marnier. This infuriates the purists but does give a slightly richer, deeper flavour.

50ml (1¾fl oz) cognac
25ml (1fl oz) triple sec
25ml (1fl oz) fresh lemon juice
Granulated sugar (optional)
Twist of lemon peel

Shake all the wet ingredients over ice and strain into a frozen martini glass. If you've got the patience you can frost the rim of the glass with sugar. Serve with a twist of lemon.

MARGARITA
TEQUILA

There are hundreds of different variations of Margarita but let's stick with the original here. If you want to jazz it up or switch it around, then be my guest. At the very least, if you want to substitute Grand Marnier or – even better in this instance – Clément Créole Shrubb Liqueur d'Orange for the triple sec, go right ahead.

50ml (1¾fl oz) blanco tequila
25ml (1fl oz) triple sec
25ml (1fl oz) fresh lime juice
Wedge of lime
Salt

Shake the tequila, triple sec and lime juice over ice and strain into a Margarita glass (if you have one), martini glass or champagne coupe, the rim rubbed with a wedge of lime and frosted with salt.

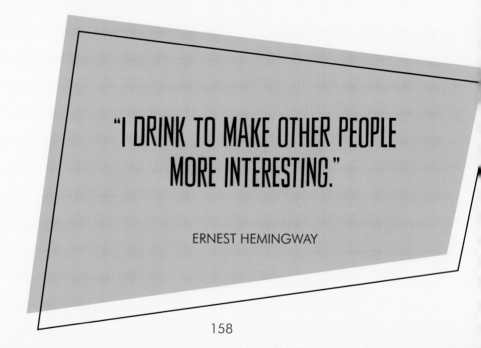

"I DRINK TO MAKE OTHER PEOPLE MORE INTERESTING."

ERNEST HEMINGWAY

THE DAIQUIRI/THE MOJITO

RUM

If ever you make it to Havana, do head across Parque Central to Floridita for a Daiquiri. A bronze statue of Ernest Hemingway – whose favourite watering hole this was – stands in mid-anecdote at one end of the bar and it was he of course who helped popularize this fabulous drink. In fact, although Floridita proclaims itself 'Cradle of the Daiquiri' and must be visited, I think those served at Havana's Hotel Nacional are rather better. Try both and see what you think. And until you do, make your own. It's so easy. Add some mint leaves and top up with soda water and you have a Mojito.

60ml (2fl oz) light rum (out of courtesy it really should be Havana Club Añejo Especial)
30ml (1fl oz) fresh lime juice
20ml (4 tsp) sugar syrup
Slice of lime

Shake all the ingredients except the slice of lime over ice, strain into a frozen martini glass and serve with the slice of lime.

THE NEGRONI

This famously fine and famously potent cocktail – half drink,
half rocket propellant – is a cinch to make and requires just
three ingredients in equal measures. You need really fine
gin though and a first-rate sweet red vermouth to go with
the Campari. But fret not, if you've only got cheap gin and
cheap vermouth, it'll still taste pretty darn good. And you can
ring the changes by using rum or absinthe instead of the gin
or even Prosecco instead of the gin in which case the drink
becomes a Sbagliato or 'mistaken' Negroni. Leave out the
gin and top up with soda water in a highball glass and you
get a refreshing Americano.

25ml (1fl oz) gin
25ml (1fl oz) Campari
25ml (1fl oz) sweet red vermouth
Strip of orange zest

Mix the gin, Campari and vermouth in a tumbler filled with
ice. Stir and serve with a zest of orange.

THE CAIPIRINHA
CACHAÇA

This is one of the simplest of all cocktails to make and one of the most delicious and rewarding, guaranteed to have you grinning from ear to ear from the very first sip. It's also great fun to muck around with by substituting all manner of fresh fruit juices for the traditional lime juice. Try muddled strawberries for instance, watermelon, orange and grated fresh ginger or even coconut milk.

2 tsp caster (superfine) sugar
1 lime, cut into eighths
50ml (1¾fl oz) cachaça

Place the sugar and the segments of lime into a tumbler and muddle them until you can squeeze no more juice out of the fruit and all the sugar is dissolved. Add the cachaça and plenty of crushed ice and stir, serving with a couple of straws.

FISH HOUSE PUNCH
RUM

Everyone has their own take on the rum punch and that's part of the fun. You can chuck in just about anything you like so long as it ends up balanced. Bear in mind, though, that a poorly made rum punch can be too watery, too sweet or too fiery.

Whilst visiting Mount Gay's distillery on Barbados I was taught their mantra for the perfect punch: one of sour, two of sweet, three of strong and four of weak. In other words, one measure of fresh lemon or lime juice, two of fruit purée or simple syrup such as grenadine, three of rum or other strong liquor, four of soda water or lemonade. Oh, and don't forget that for variety, the three parts strong can include three different rums or three different spirits altogether.

Funnily enough, though, the most memorable rum punch I ever had was in the fabulous Helvetica Bar in Perth, Western Australia and I am indebted to them for allowing me to reprint their Fish House Punch recipe here. I'm told that it dates from 1732 when members of the Schuylkill Fishing Co in Philadelphia concocted a rum punch for their Christmas party that would titillate their lady guests' palates whilst also getting them a bit livelier than was usual.

60ml (2fl oz) Angostura 5 Year Old Rum
30ml (1fl oz) Martell VS Cognac
30ml (1fl oz) peach liqueur
30ml (1fl oz) sugar syrup
45ml (1½fl oz) fresh lemon juice
100ml (3½fl oz) soda water
5 fresh peach slices
5 lemon slices
60ml (2fl oz) sparkling wine

Add all the ingredients bar the sparkling wine to a large jug (pitcher) or jar and stir well over ice. Then top up with the fizz. Serves 2–4.

THE MINT JULEP
BOURBON

Everyone loves a Mint Julep. It's both deeply refreshing and –
so long as you don't leave it too long in the sun thus allowing
the ice to melt and dilute the drink – pleasantly alcoholic. It's
also dead easy to make.

1 tsp caster (superfine) sugar or sugar syrup
Several sprigs of fresh mint (traditionally spearmint)
50ml (1¾fl oz) fine bourbon

Muddle the sugar and the mint in the bottom of a pewter cup,
highball or Old Fashioned glass. Fill with crushed or shaved
ice, add the bourbon and serve with a straw and an extra
sprig of mint.

ESTRELLITA: Ma'am, did he hear that or did he smell it?
NORA CHARLES: That's Mr. Charles, isn't it?
ESTRELLITA: Yes'm.
NORA CHARLES: This is a cocktail, isn't it?
ESTRELLITA: Yes'm.
NORA CHARLES: They'll get together.
(From: *Shadow of the Thin Man*, 1941)

THE 100 SPIRITS, BY TYPE

ARMAGNAC

Domaine Boingnères Bas Armagnac Cépages Nobles	33
Darroze Les Grands Assemblages 12 Year Old Armagnac	52
Janneau Grand Armagnac VSOP	89
Château de Laubade XO Bas Armagnac	102

CALVADOS, APPLE BRANDY & FRUIT BRANDY

Didier Lemorton Réserve Domfrontais Calvados	55
Jean-Paul Metté Eau-de-Vie de Poire Williams	90
Somerset Cider Brandy 10 Year Old	132

OTHER BRANDY

1615 Pisco Pura Italia	131

GRAPPA

Bottega Riserva Privata Barricata Grappa	34
Nardini Grappa Mandorla	114

RUM & CACHAÇA

Mount Gay XO Rum	113
Santa Teresa 1796 Rum	130
Chairman's Reserve Rum, The Forgotten Casks	42
Havana Club Añejo Especial Rum	81
Appleton Estate 21 Year Old Rum	18
El Dorado 15 Year Old Special Reserve Rum	59
Foursquare Spiced Rum	63
Magnífica de Faria Cachaça	105

TEQUILA

Gran Patrón Platinum Silver Tequila	75
Ocho Reposado Single Estate Tequila	117
Tapatio Añejo Tequila	143

MEZCAL

Derrumbes Oaxaca Joven Mezcal	54

VODKA

Absolut Elyx Single Estate Handcrafted Vodka	12
Belvedere Single Estate Rye Vodka	24
Ketel One Citroen Vodka	96
Ramsbury Single Estate Vodka	123
Spirit of Hven Organic Summer Spirit	135

GIN & JENEVER

Beefeater 24 Gin	22
Berrys' No. 3 Gin	30
Bobby's Schiedam Jenever	32
Brighton Gin	35
Copper Rivet Dockyard Gin	47
Foxdenton Winslow Plum Gin	64
Isle of Harris Gin	87
Ki No Bi Kyoto Dry Gin	97
The Story Gin	137
Tanqueray No. Ten Gin	139

SOJU

Jinro 24 Soju	92

ABSINTHE

Versinthe La Blanche Absinthe	145

WHERE TO BUY FINE SPIRITS

UK

BERRY BROS & RUDD
3 St. James's Street
London SW1A 1EG
www.bbr.com

D. BYRNE & CO
Victoria Buildings
12 King Street
Clitheroe
Lancashire BB7 2EP
www.dbyrne-finewines.co.uk

GERRY'S WINES & SPIRITS
74 Old Compton Street
London W1D 4UW
www.gerrys.uk.com

HEDONISM WINES
3-7 Davies Street
London W1K 3LD
www.hedonism.co.uk

LEA & SANDEMAN
170 Fulham Road
London SW10 9PR
www.leaandsandeman.co.uk

LUVIANS BOTTLESHOP
93 Bonnygate
Cupar
Fife KY15 4LG
www.luvians.com

MASTER OF MALT
Unit 5
Chapman Way
Royal Tunbridge Wells
Kent TN2 3EF
www.masterofmalt.com

TANNERS
26 Wyle Cop
Shrewsbury
Shropshire SY1 1XD
www.tanners-wines.co.uk

THE WHISKY EXCHANGE
2 Bedford Street
London WC2E 9HH
www.thewhiskyexchange.
com

YAPP BROTHERS
Mere
Wilts BA12 6DY
www.yapp.co.uk

AUSTRALIA

PRINCE WINE STORE
166 Bank Street
South Melbourne 3205

40 Hansard Street
Zetland 2017

80 Primrose Street
Essendon 3181
www.princewinestore.com.
au

EAST END CELLARS
25 Vardon Avenue
Adelaide 5000
www.eastendcellars.com.au

FIRST CHOICE LIQUOR
www.firstchoiceliquor.com.
au

NEW ZEALAND

GLENGARRY
www.glengarrywines.co.nz

HANCOCKS
www.hancocks.co.nz

USA

BEVMO!
www.bevmo.com

TOTAL WINE & MORE
www.totalwine.com

LIQUOR BARN
www.theliquorbarn.com

CANADA

BC LIQUOR STORES
www.bcliquorstores.com

**LIQUOR CONTROL
BOARD OF ONTARIO**
www.LCBO.com

INDEX

Publishing Director Sarah Lavelle
Commissioning Editor Céline Hughes
Designers Gemma Hayden, Nicola Ellis
Picture Researcher Samantha Rolfe-Hoang
Illustrator David Doran
Production Controller Tom Moore
Production Director Vincent Smith

Published in 2018 by Quadrille,
an imprint of Hardie Grant Publishing

Quadrille
52–54 Southwark Street
London SE1 1UN
quadrille.com

Cataloguing in Publication Data:
A catalogue record for this book is
available from the British Library.

ISBN 978 178713 264 1

Reprinted in 2018
10 9 8 7 6 5 4 3 2

Printed and bound in China

Picture Credits

p41 Mary Evans Picture Library/Onslow Auctions Limited; p82 © The Russell Butcher
Collection/Mary Evans Picture Library; p95 credit courtesy of the Diageo Archive; p121
Mary Evans/Grenville Collins Postcard Collection; p147 © Illustrated London News
Ltd/Mary Evans; p155 Mary Evans Picture Library; p161 Bitter Campari Aperitif (1957);
Carlo Fisanotti (alias Fisa); p165 Mary Evans Picture Library.

Every effort has been made to trace the copyright holders of the material published in
this book. We apologize if any material has been reproduced without permission.

ACKNOWLEDGEMENTS

Getting paid to drink and then write about it is a ridiculous and often shambolic way to earn a living. That I ever managed to get this book started, let alone finished, is thanks largely to the invaluable encouragement and help I received from individuals at the many drinks companies mentioned in these pages – far too many, unfortunately, to thank by name.

I would, though, like to single out and thank Céline Hughes – the most patient of editors – for entrusting me with this book and for coming up with the perfect title. I'd also like to thank David Doran for his excellent cover, Gemma Hayden for making the book look so gorgeous, Tom Moore for his sterling production skills, Katie Read for kindly taking on the publicity and Quadrille's UK Sales Team for being so keen on the idea from the start.

My old chums Dave Broom and Dawn Davies MW have both been typically selfless and generous with their time and advice and Judith Murray remains the most supportive of literary agents.

It goes without saying that any mistakes still lurking in the book are down to my own chronic laziness and incompetence rather than anybody else's.

And finally, love and thanks to my wife Marina, the most stalwart of drinking companions whose deft mastery of the Boston shaker never fails to impress.